DAYLIGHTING DESIGN

Planning Strategies
and Best Practice Solutions

To
Elyes Adam and Yanis Emile

To
my mother and my late father

MOHAMED BOUBEKRI

DAYLIGHTING DESIGN

Planning Strategies
and Best Practice Solutions

With an Introduction by
Christian Bartenbach and Mohamed Boubekri

BIRKHÄUSER
BASEL

Layout, cover design
and typesetting:
Reinhard Steger
Deborah van Mourik
Proxi, Barcelona

Library of Congress Catalog-
ing-in-Publication data
A CIP catalog record for this
book has been applied for at the
Library of Congress.

Bibliographic information published by the German National
Library
The German National Library
lists this publication in the
Deutsche Nationalbibliografie;
detailed bibliographic data
are available on the Internet at
http://dnb.dnb.de.

This publication is also available
as an e-book
(ISBN PDF 978-3-03821-478-6;
ISBN EPUB 978-3-03821-688-9).

© 2014 Birkhäuser Verlag GmbH,
Basel
P.O. Box 44, 4009 Basel,
Switzerland
Part of Walter de Gruyter GmbH
Berlin/Boston

Printed on acid-free paper produced from chlorine-free pulp.
TCF ∞

Printed in Germany

ISBN 978-3-7643-7728-1

9 8 7 6 5 4 3 2 1

www.birkhauser.com

About the Author

Dr. Mohamed Boubekri is a professor of architecture at the University of Illinois at Urbana-Champaign. He is a William Wayne Caudill Research Fellow, and twice a Fulbright Fellow. He received his first professional degree in architecture from the Université des Sciences et Technologie d'Oran, Algeria; a second professional master's degree from the University of Colorado-Denver, and a PhD from Texas A&M University. His teaching has encompassed such areas as architectural design, building illumination, architectural acoustics, building economics, daylighting design, energy and building performance assessments. He has taught in several institutions around the world including Canada, Kuwait, United Arab Emirates, and the United States. Professor Boubekri's research focuses on sustainable architecture and the intersection of the built environment and human health and well-being. He has published more than 70 journal articles and conferences papers. His first book, published in 2008, explores the impact of daylighting of buildings on people's health and overall well-being. More generally, his work also examines the relationship between architectural design, sustainable technologies, and building energy/environmental performance.

Acknowledgements

I would like to thank the Research Board of the University of Illinois at Urbana-Champaign (UIUC), the College of Fine and Applied Arts for their financial support without which this project would not have been possible. I would like to acknowledge the many individuals and organizations, who are too many to name here, who have very generously provided me with illustrations and information vital for this project. I am especially appreciative of the contribution of Bartenbach GmbH from Innsbruck, Austria, especially Wilfried Pohl, for his support and contributions without which this book could not have been realized in the manner that it did. I am honored and grateful to have Professor Christian Bartenbach co-write the introduction chapter of this book.
I would like to thank my graduate research assistant, Thulasi Ram Khamma for helping me with many illustrations.
I would like to thank Henriette Mueller-Stahl from Birkhäuser for being the best editor any author would dream to have.
I am especially indebted to my friend and colleague, Gaines B. Hall, for his advice, patience, friendship, and for editing twice this entire manuscript.
I am very grateful to all my family for their unremitting support.
I am forever beholden to my mother and late father for their limitless sacrifice.
Last but not least, I am very thankful beyond words to my two angels, Adam Elyes and Emile Yanis, for their unconditional love and for truly making me a very happy dad.

TABLE OF CONTENTS

CHAPTER 1

INTRODUCTION

BY CHRISTIAN BARTENBACH AND MOHAMED BOUBEKRI

Historical Perspective

But the architects who are designing rooms today have lost faith in natural light. By becoming dependent on the light switch they are content with static light and forget about the endlessly changing character of natural light which transforms a room each second of the day.

Louis Kahn, (*Stille und Licht*, i.e. "silence and light"), lecture at School of Architecture of the Eidgenössische Technische Hochschule, Zurich, February 12, 1969).

The history of daylighting is the history of architecture. Sunlight has warmed human habitat since the beginning and has remained a primary factor in the design of habitations. Incorporating sunlight into structures was a fundamental design element in the buildings of many civilizations. Long ago, when buildings were illuminated by torches and fireplaces, building concepts were formulated with daylight in mind. The natural incidence of light and the transparency of a structure for natural light were essential elements in these concepts. Architecture of ancient civilizations such as those of the Persians, the Arabs, the Greeks, and the Romans featured dwellings modeled around a courtyard that welcomed natural light, tempered the harsh climate outside, and became the hub of the house. The Greeks believed in democratizing solar access in their town planning as was apparent in the model communities of Olynthus and Priene. The Romans pioneered the idea of solar zoning legislation that allowed citizens access to the sun in their dwellings. In the second century, a legal precedent for solar rights was established and later was included in the Roman Justinian Code of Law. The writings of Vitruvius, the eminent Roman architect in the first century B.C., influenced architects for centuries to come, including Palladio from the Renaissance period up to the modern age. In his *Ten Books of Architecture*, in Book 1, Chapter 2, "The Five Fundamental Principles of Architecture", Vitruvius wrote:

There will also be natural propriety in using an eastern light for bedrooms and libraries, a western light in winter for baths and winter apartments, and a northern light for picture galleries and other places in which a steady light is needed; for that quarter of the sky grows neither light nor dark with the course of the sun, but remains steady and unshifting all day long.[1]
Vitruvius, 2002

The history of daylighting is closely related to the history of technological developments of human civilization. While the Romanesque churches were dark and grim inside because of the massive load-bearing masonry walls and the short spans above their fenestration, the advent of the flying buttresses as structural features during the gothic era relieved the requirement to support the entire structural load with the walls and allowed gothic structures to admit much more daylight than their romanesque counterparts.

Later, in 1781, James Watt patented the first steam engine in human history. The creation of the steam engine was a catalyst to the industrial revolution that changed so many aspects of human life. In the mid-18th century, the world experienced massive migrations of people looking for work in manufacturing from rural areas to urban centers, particularly in Western Europe. This phenomenon of affordable, fast mass transportation produced enormous economic, social, and architectural changes. Skyrocketing demands for housing due to the rapid and large influx of populations led to overcrowded and unsanitary ghettos in many cities in Great Britain, Western Europe, and North America. Migrant workers found shelter in densely populated buildings, built back-to-back along narrow streets with poor sanitary conditions, and with open sewers and little or no exposure to daylight. Architects produced cheap and expedient solutions for an emerging housing shortage but with little thought to the undesirable and unhealthy living conditions into which the people were being placed.

Awareness of the importance of light in people's lives grew when Dr. Niels Finson received the Nobel Prize in 1903 for proving that sunlight could cure tuberculosis (Holick, 2004). The early part of the 20th century witnessed the beginning of new Modern Architecture movement that embraced modernity and rejected the old ways of designing buildings. Until then, buildings had been pastiches of past styles. They were dark and unhealthy with massive masonry structures and small windows. Technological advances spurred new ways of thinking about building design. Buildings could now be constructed with long spans and large openings. This new architecture emphasized straight lines and simple, economic forms, and incorporated large expanses of windows that maximized natural light and fresh air. Human scale, along with principles of proportion and ergonomics, became key principles in building design. This new architecture was concerned with economy, hygiene, health, and the natural environment. *La Ville Radieuse* and *L'esprit Nouveau* of Le Corbusier were quintessential paradigms of this new and modern way of thinking about designing new buildings and new cities that emphasized green spaces and access to sunlight for the benefit of the inhabitants. Many master architects have used daylight as a primary design element in their architecture. *"Architecture is the masterly, correct, and magnificent play of masses brought together under the light,"* said Le Corbusier (Le Corbusier, 2007).

1.1 - *La Ville Radieuse* concept of Le Corbusier

Citing Louis Kahn: "As soon as I see a plan which tries to sell me spaces without light, I simply reject it with such an ease, as though it were not even thoughtfully rejected, because I know it is wrong. And so, false prophets, like schools that have no natural light, are definitely un-architectural. Those are what I like to call – belong to the marketplace of architecture but not to architecture itself." (Latour, 1991).

While this nascent and refreshing way of thinking about architecture was taking hold in the early part of the 20th century in Europe and North America, other technological developments were occurring simultaneously. The development of fluorescent lighting technology in the 1920s meant that buildings could be illuminated relatively cheaply compared to the electric lighting technology that previously existed. The successful commercialization of the fluorescent lighting technology in the 1930s constituted a significant setback for the cause of daylighting. Fluorescent lighting allowed buildings to have large floor plates and be lit fairly cheaply without relying on windows and natural light. This new lighting technology was a major improvement in terms of energy efficiency compared to incandescent lighting which became the primary artificial light source with Thomas Edison's first incandescent lamp in 1876. With increased pressure from utility companies to increase the consumption of electricity, architects were urged to rely increasingly on fluorescent light for building illumination. Economies of structure encouraged the lowering of ceilings, thereby reducing the volume of the building to be heated or cooled but also reducing the penetration of daylight. Because of the practicality of fluorescent lighting, many building professionals even argued that daylight was a luxury that could be disregarded altogether since fluorescent

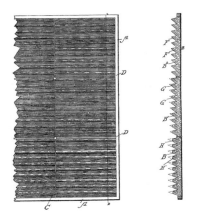

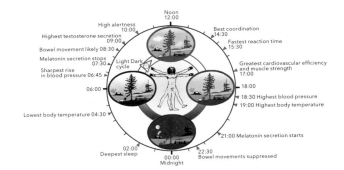

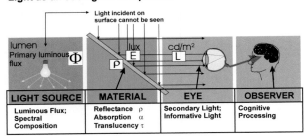

1.2 – Glass light-channeling devices from 1890 to 1930

1.3 – Typical human "circadian biological clock" with some physiological parameters.

1.4 – Primary light – secondary light – perception

lighting could supply ample light adequately and economically. The innovation in prism glass 1.2, used from 1890 to 1930 in a number of buildings in North America and Europe, was an attempt to restore some of what was lost in terms of daylighting potential of these new buildings with low ceilings. The technology of prism glass allowed daylight to be redirected from the window wall location to the back area of the room allowing rooms to be deeper and with higher daylight levels in the back. According to recommendations and architectural practices of those times, it was no longer necessary to have a courtyard for core daylighting. Now it was possible to eliminate inner courtyards and increase the rentable space.

Application handbooks on the subject of prismatic glazing were published, and Frank Lloyd Wright provided the industry with expert advice and numerous applications by way of his designed projects.

The 1973 energy crisis was a watershed moment for many aspects of our lives including architectural research and practice. Ever since that crisis, a worldwide awakening occurred that recognized the amount of energy we consume in buildings. This energy crisis powerfully illustrated the blend of environmentalism with concerns over resource scarcity. The quality of our lives and human comfort was no longer inseparable from our energy resources. The solar architecture initiative of the late 1970s and early 1980s, arguably the basis of today's green architectural practices, was a direct consequence of the 1973 oil embargo.

Today's Perspective

Recent efforts worldwide to decrease the energy consumption in buildings (e.g., net- zero energy buildings targets in the European Union, or the *2030 Challenge*, or *Leadership in Energy & Environmental Design (LEED)* in the United States) brought daylighting and energy conservation back into focus. The recent concerns about global warming put the discourse about green architecture at the forefront of architectural research and practice. Until recently, design practices related to energy conservation always were measured against economic benchmarks. Today, we are not concerned just about saving energy in order to spend less. We also are concerned about reducing the consumption of fossil energy which is measured by the reduction of CO_2 emissions and the lasting impact on the environment.

Over the last decade, there has been a growing awareness and a body of research about the impact of the built environment on people's health and well-being. How the health of building occupants is influenced by building design is, however, no longer thought of only in terms of the sick building syndrome paradigm which focuses almost exclusively on indoor air quality issues. Today, the discussion of the influence of building design on people's health deals with almost all aspects of the building environment including heat, light, sound, and air quality. Physical and psychological health is deemed important not only for moral arguments but because of economic reasons. Productivity, absenteeism, and scholastic performance can be positively influenced by how a building is designed when the health and well-being of the occupants is a primary design goal.

With the realization that people spend the great majority of their lifetime indoors (some say 90%), it is no longer possible to ignore the role that architecture plays in promoting or degrading people's health. The quality of life can be enhanced significantly by improving people's visual, biological, and thermal environment through a number of design considerations including daylighting. The visual environment relates to the proper conditions for good visual perception, comfort, and performance – important design elements in workplace environments. The biological environment represents the non-visual effects of daylight, such as those relating to the production of the serotonin and melatonin hormones that regulate our vital circadian rhythm [1.3]. Seasonal affective disorder (SAD) is a well-known consequence of insufficient daylight exposure and a disturbance of the serotonin/melatonin cycle.

Daylight is also crucial for our production of vitamin D, the lack of which is known to contribute to many diseases such as rickets, osteomalacia, depression, and possibly different types of internal cancers. The lifestyle of modern man leads to a lack of daylight and sunlight exposure and an overexposure to artificial light at night. This condition decouples our lives from the cyclical rhythms of the natural environment. Researchers call this decoupling process chronodisruption. For several years, medical researchers

from such disciplines as occupational medicine, oncology, neurology, and chronobiology have been investigating the medium- to long-term effects of this decoupling process. Today, it is believed that long-term chronodisruption could contribute to a significant reduction of neuropsychological capabilities, sleep disturbances, and disorders of the cardiovascular system. In 2007 the International Agency for Research on Cancer (IARC), a branch agency of the World Health Organization, classified long-term shift work as a contributor to chronodisruption and potentially carcinogenic to humans.

Light as a Medium

For human beings and other life forms, light is the most important medium for transmitting visual information about the environment. The information capacity of daylight consists of its intensity, spectral composition, temporal character, the sense of orientation it provides, the sense of spatial depth one gets from its spatial distribution, and the existence of shadows. Primary light is the component of daylight that is invisible and one that does not bear information [1.4]. In the same way that a series of letters turns into information through systematic structuring, light is endowed with its information structure only when it comes into contact with an object through reflection, absorption, and transmission. Primary light is the main agent of illumination, and not the resulting effect of the act of illumination. The effective light, the component that makes objects visible, is the secondary or environmental light.

For the most part, secondary light is the reflected component that enters the eye as a modulated form of the primary light and makes an object identifiable. The qualitative variety of the secondary light can only evolve according to the inherent possibilities of primary light. In this regard, daylight possesses the highest potential for containing information about the environment. With daylight as a primary light, the temporal character of daylight and its continuous changes influence the secondary light in a unique way that cannot be obtained under electric light. Due to the large distance between the earth and the sun, sun rays reaching the surface of the earth are nearly parallel. However, the angle of incidence is subject to ongoing changes that differ with time and place and follow the laws of nature; these changes are characteristics of daylight and thus distinguish it from artificial light.

Sunbeams are refracted when they enter the atmosphere. The degree of light diffusion depends on the local composition of the penetrated medium.

With regard to time and place, the changes in the atmosphere are largely manifested in the climate; regionally, they are evident in the form of different weather conditions which influence intensity, spectral power distribution, and directness of sunlight. Many periodic cycles in nature and man (seasons, alternation of day and night, etc.) result from the fluctuations of daylight according to the laws of nature.

Under clear skies, daylight provides an illuminance of up to 100,000 lux and a strict directness which is visible in its strong contrasts and the sharpness of shadows. Under cloudy or foggy conditions, the level of illuminance reaches only a fraction of this amount (1/5th to 1/10th); the light is completely diffused and a state of shadowlessness occurs.

The primary spectrum of the sun is changed by absorption and scattering when the radiation passes through the atmosphere, representing the daylight with which we are familiar. The sky changes its colors from the crystal blue of midday to the flaming red of sunset to the "blue hour" twilight in the evening, and the darkness of night. The original structure of the sunlight spectrum exhibits a maximum of energy in the blue-green area, whereas the energy peak of the terrestrial sunlight is shifted to the yellow-green wavelengths. With its luminance of about 10^9 candela/m^2 (cd/m^2), the sun outshines all artificial light sources. Its energy on earth measures between 600 and 1000 Watts/m^2 (W/m^2). The ratio between the horizontal and vertical illuminance components presents a unique characteristic for daylighting. When the sun is at a medium to high altitude angle, the vertical illumination amounts to 40% to 60% of the horizontal illumination. When the sun is at a low altitude angle, the vertical illumination predominates, thereby giving objects an appearance different from that caused by a high sun. This changing, rich, and complex behavior of daylight is essential for our visual, psychological, and biological needs.

Lighting Design – A Contemplation

Nature in the form of water, light and sky restores architecture from a metaphysical to an earthly plane and gives life to architecture.
Ando, 1991

Modern buildings are often open to daylight in the sense that they use extended glass facades. The U.S. Department of Energy released some statistics citing that 35% of the current building stock in the United States has sufficient glass facades to benefit from daylighting. If all these buildings were equipped with photocells that control the electrical lighting system, the United States would be saving annually 8,112 Megawatts, the equivalent of four times the annual energy production of Hoover Dam.

Daylighting does not necessarily entail having glass facades all over our buildings. An all-glass building with no daylighting controls may experience more problems than benefits in the form of excessive solar heat gain, overheating, and extreme glare problems. Daylighting is about the judicious quantitative and qualitative control of the daylight inside a building. Daylighting is about the careful study of a building's positioning within its site and microclimate, a proper shape, orientation, and fenestration so that it is able to meet many requirements, which seem contradictory at times. 1.5 Generally speaking these requirements are:

- increasing daylight levels in the core area of the building
- having the right amount of daylight for the appropriate time duration
- protecting the occupants against excessive glare
- allowing a good view to the outside
- minimizing solar heat gain in the summer while maximizing it in winter.

Light and Human Perception

The images in 1.6 do not have the same foreground light. Note the color of the hair and dress and the shadows on them. There is more that is different than the backgrounds.

Lighting design is more than the planning of stipulated light intensities and illuminance levels. It is also more than the fulfillment of physiological visual requirements for visual task performance. The fulfillment of these requirements resides as a necessary prerequisite to proper illumination. Lighting design has a greater mission than the simple fulfillment of normative guidelines. It is about the fulfillment of these basic requirements while being mindful of the emotional, psychological, and aesthetic needs of the user. Some of these human factors are not yet fully understood but merit investigation and consideration nevertheless. Issues of spectral composition, luminance contrasts, light intensity, and color are intricately related in defining the appearance of an object or a room. These considerations are not always fulfilled by applying technical concepts or mathematical algorithms.

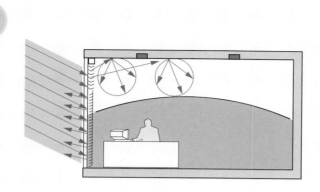

1.5 – Basic requirements for daylighting
1.6 – Comparison of two different backgrounds
(© Bartenbach GmbH)

1.6

CHAPTER 2

ECONOMICS OF DAYLIGHTING

Daylighting and Energy Costs

The world energy use is growing at an alarming rate and is raising concerns about the depletion of energy resources. According to the International Energy Agency (IEA, 2012), primary energy, i.e., energy that has not been subjected to any transformation process, has grown by 49% and CO_2 emissions by 43% during the period between 1984 and 2011 2.1. With the economic growth of the underdeveloped world, consumption is expected to increase at a much higher rate than what we have witnessed to date 2.2. The building sector has a very important role to play in making significant changes in the energy use in the future. Buildings account for more than 40% of the energy consumption and more than 45% of the CO_2 emissions 2.3, 2.4. In Japan, buildings consume more than 50% of all the energy produced. According to the 2008 report by the U.S. Department of Energy (US DOE, 2008), the growth in the energy consumption of buildings comes predominantly from electricity. Electricity's share of primary energy use in buildings in the United States increased from 56% in 1980 to 72% in 2005. U.S. electricity use in 2011 was more than 13 times greater than electricity use in 1950. In 1995, electricity usage accounted for 88% of energy cost in office buildings in 1995, and 63% of energy costs in all buildings in 2012. The U.S. Energy Information Agency (US EIA, 2013) estimates that in 2011, about 461 billion kilowatt-hours (kWh) of electricity were used for lighting by the residential and commercial sectors. This electricity usage was equal to about 17% of the total electricity consumed by both of these sectors and about 12% of total U.S. electricity consumption.

Residential lighting consumption was about 186 billion kWh, or 13% of all residential electricity consumption in the U.S. The commercial sector, which includes commercial and institutional buildings, public streets and highway lighting, consumed about 275 billion kWh for lighting, or 21% of commercial sector electricity consumption in 2011.

One of the earliest and most powerful arguments in favor of daylighting is its potential to reduce the reliance on electricity for building illumination. Growing concerns about the depletion of fossil energy sources and climate change have put today's energy efficiency at the core of architectural practice and research. How much electric energy consumption can be reduced by daylight depends largely on the daylighting strategies adopted.

What is certain is that daylighting has a tremendous potential to reduce energy consumption and CO_2 emissions. According to the Industry & University Cooperative Research Program of the National Science Foundation in the U.S. Center for Building Performance and Diagnostics at Carnegie Mellon University (NSF/IUCRC, 2004), with a total area of approximately 1.11 billion m², U.S. office buildings use over 86 billion kWh of electricity for lighting each year. It is estimated that 35% of office buildings, as currently designed, have sufficient fenestration and are appropriately massed and glazed for daylighting. At an average energy cost of $0.08 per kWh, the potential savings from lighting energy reductions due to implementing high performance daylighting in those 35% of office buildings is more than $1.25 billion/year, equivalent to over 15.6 billion kWh of saved energy annually. To put things in a palpable perspective, these potential energy savings would be equivalent to the annual production of nearly four Hoover Dams, or to the annual energy consumption of 577,800 households (nearly half the size of Los Angeles, CA), or to the annual gasoline energy use of 778,700 cars in the U.S. (NSF/IUCRC, 2004)

Lowering the electric energy used for building illumination also can reduce the large amount of heat produced by the electric light sources and consequently decrease a building's cooling loads. There are other substantial economic incentives of daylighting that relate to lowering peak demand besides total energy consumption. Lowering peak demand is especially important in commercial and office buildings that are daytime-occupied, and for which peak demand occurs during the time when daylight is the most abundant 2.6. For these types of buildings the cost of energy is due primarily to their electric power demand, not only the energy consumption. In fact, the demand charges can far outweigh the energy consumption charges. Projections show that total electricity and peak demand savings of 20% to 40% in lighting and its related cooling energy can be achieved with the proper use of photosensors and automatic lighting controls. A study in Hong Kong showed that it is even possible to reduce not only site energy consumption but also power plant capacity by adopting daylighting controls (Li, 2005). This study indicated that the reductions for the maximum cooling plant load and building electrical demand for the base-case model due to daylighting were 5% and 9.3%, respectively 2.5.

2.1

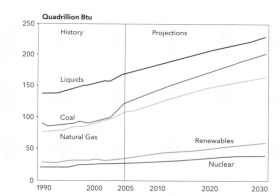

2.2

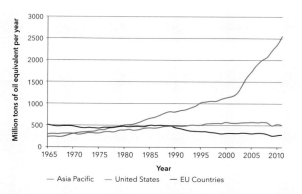

2.1 – World energy use by fuel type (Source: United States Energy Information Agency, 2008)

2.2 – Coal consumption in Asia Pacific, U.S. and EU countries between 1965 and 2011

2.3 – U.S. energy consumption by sector (Source: United States Energy Information Administration, 2011)

2.4 – U.S. CO_2 emission by sector (Source: United States Energy Information Administration, 2011)

2.3

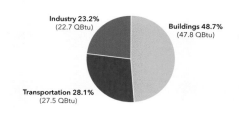

Industry 23.2% (22.7 QBtu)
Buildings 48.7% (47.8 QBtu)
Transportation 28.1% (27.5 QBtu)

2.4

Industry 19.9% (1120 MMT CO2e)
Buildings 46.7% (2631 MMT CO2e)
Transportation 33.4% (1881 MMT CO2e)

Significant progress has been achieved over the last two decades in improving the energy efficiency of electric light sources. Even with the availability of additional energy efficient lamps, electronic ballasts, and alternative control systems, the cost saving potential for daylighting is substantial. The U.S. building sector's energy consumption is expected to increase 35% between 2013 and 2025; commercial energy demand is projected to grow at an average annual rate of 1.6%, reaching 25.3 quads (or ~7,413 billion Kwh) in 2025. The quad is a unit used by the U.S. Department of Energy in discussing world and national energy budgets. There is an acute urgency to develop and deploy emerging energy-efficient technologies that can deliver reliable energy and peak demand reductions throughout the lifespan of a building while contributing to the comfort, satisfaction, and productivity of the building occupants. Daylighting technologies certainly are at the vanguard of these emerging technologies. The last two decades have been the theater of applications of many such technologies.

The new corporate headquarters of the New York Times Company was designed to promote "transparency" to the public via floor-to-ceiling clear glass windows shaded by a unique exterior shading system 2.7. Since the building's opening in 2007, a collaborative research partnership was created between the Lawrence Berkeley National Laboratory (LBNL), industry, and public funding agencies to conduct a monitored field test to evaluate

several commercially-available automated facade-daylighting systems. The curtain wall, fully glazed with low-e glass, maximizes natural light within the building while the ceramic-rod screen helps to shade from direct sunlight and reduce cooling loads. The daylighting strategy coupled with the use of more than 18,000 individually dimmable fluorescent fixtures supplement natural light, providing real energy savings of 30%. Measured results from the post-occupancy monitored evaluation in the final building showed a 24% reduction in annual electricity use and a 51% reduction in heating energy use five years after initial occupancy, compared to initial expectations from a design that met only the baseline energy-efficiency code (ASHRAE 90.1-2001), and a 25% reduction in peak electric demand. The company's investment is estimated to yield a 12% rate of return on their initial investment (Lawrence Berkeley National Labs, 2013).

Another example of successful daylighting strategies is the Harmony Library in Fort Collins, Colorado. Winner of the 2001 Colorado Renewable Energy Society (CRES) Renewable Energy in Buildings Awards, it achieved a 36% energy savings according to measurements performed by researchers from the Lighting Research Center of the Rensselaer Polytechnic Institute (LRC, 2004). The daylighting strategy relies on high clerestory windows surrounding the stacks and reading areas and on side windows along the peripheral walls of the library 2.8, 2.9. Daylight sensors control the ambient lighting fixtures near

2.5

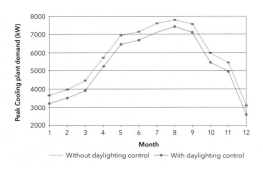

2.5 – Monthly peak cooling plant capacity in a Hong Kong study (Courtesy: Elsevier)

2.6 – Peak demand occurrence (Source: Lawrence Berkley National Laboratories)

2.6

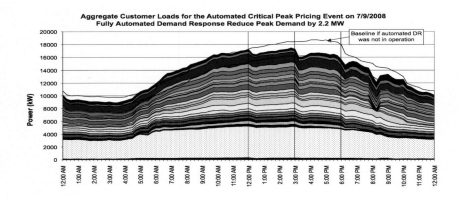

2.7 – New York Times building in New York City, USA (Photo: M. Boubekri)
2.8 – Exterior view of the Harmony Library in Fort Collins, USA (Photo courtesy: Annie Fox)
2.9 – Interior view of the Harmony Library in Fort Collins, USA (Photo courtesy: Annie Fox)

2.8

2.9

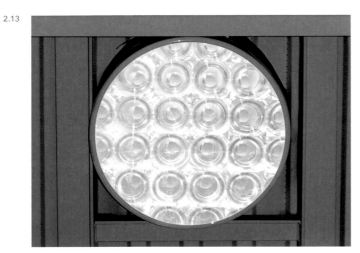

2.10 – Exterior view of the David Suzuki Public School in Windsor, Ontario, USA (Photo courtesy: Greater Essex County District School Board)

2.11 – Solar tracking skylights in the David Suzuki Public School, Canada (Photo courtesy: Greater Essex County District School Board)

2.11 – Close-up of the solar tracking skylight system used in the David Suzuki Public School, Canada (Photo courtesy: Greater Essex County District School Board)

2.13 – Diffuser of the Lightpipe system used in the David Suzuki Public School, Canada (Photo courtesy: Greater Essex County District School Board)

2.14 – Typical classroom in the David Suzuki Public School equipped with high clerestory windows and interior light-shelves, Canada (Photo courtesy: Greater Essex County District School Board)

2.15 – The Newberg Center at Portland Community College, Newberg, Oregon, USA (Photo courtesy: Nick Lehoux)

2.16 – Section across the Newberg Center showing the PV system, the natural ventilation system, and the skylight daylighting strategy used in lecture rooms, USA (Photo courtesy: Hennebery Eddy Architects)

2.17 – Skylight system at the Newberg Center, Canada (Photo courtesy: Stephen Miller)

2.18 – Large skylights used in the lecture rooms of the Newberg Center, Canada (Photo courtesy: Stephen Miller)

the clerestory and side windows, automatically turning off some light fixtures for 78% of the operating hours.

Another educational building where daylighting has received significant emphasis is the public school in Windsor, Ontario, named after the internationally renowned Canadian environmentalist Dr. David Suzuki 2.10. This school is a two-story building, where the daylight harvesting systems include skylights with sun trackers, lightpipes, clerestories, lighshelves in addition to side windows 2.11-2.14. This project received the Leadership in Energy and Environmental Design (LEED) Platinum certification from the US-Green Energy Council. The school owner's goal for this school was to showcase what can be achieved with today's technologies and incorporate the building's sustainable strategies into the school's curricula. In one year of measurements taken between September 1, 2010, and August 31, 2011, this school consumed 84 kWh/m², at a cost of approximately US $50,800. This lower energy consumption translates into annual energy cost savings of US $79,600, or 61%, compared to a comparable non-LEED school building.

Another noteworthy example is the Portland Community College (PCC) Newberg Center, featured as a "Top 10" project of The American Institute of Architects (AIA) Committee on the Environment because of design quality, innovative design, and energy-efficient building performance. The approximately 1,250m² LEED Platinum building is designed to be a Net-Zero Energy Building meaning it will meet all of its energy needs, over the course of a year, through conservation measures, on-site power generation, and successful passive design strategies. Designed by Hennebery Eddy Architects, the building makes daylighting a major design consideration 2.15-2.18. Daylighting strategy combines common skylights and acoustical ceiling tiles in a unique sloped ceiling system. Large panes of frosted glass, between the classrooms and commons, light the classrooms from two sides while north-facing clerestory windows evenly light the space. The Newberg Center was seen as a pilot project for Portland Community College (PCC) to understand sustainable building strategies. The simple payback for the proposed facility, with all net-zero aspects combined, is 20 years and 2 months without including state and federal incentives.

2.15

2.17

2.16

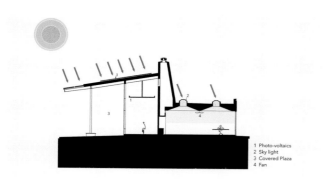

1 Photo-voltaics
2 Sky light
3 Covered Plaza
4 Fan

2.18

2.19 – South facade of three-story middle wing of the Manassas Park Elementary School, USA. "Daylight Windows" with LightLouver™ units located above the "Vision Windows," which have an overhang to reduce solar heat gain into the classrooms (Photo courtesy: Sam Kittner)

2.20 – Exterior of the Manassas Park Elementary School, USA, showing sawtooth roof monitors and solar tracking skylights for top lighting (Photo courtesy: Sam Kittner)

2.21 – Patented optical slat design of the LightLouver side-lighting system

2.22 – Close-up view of the "daylight windows" with the LightLouver units and of the horizontal lightshelf above the exterior lighshelves (Photo courtesy: Sam Kittner)

2.23 – Interior of a south facing classroom – LightLouver units in the upper "daylight windows" above the "view windows" (Photo courtesy: Sam Kittner)

2.20

2.21

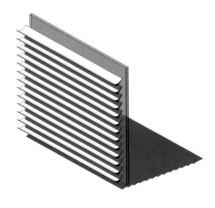

2.22

The Manassas Park Elementary School (MPES) is a 13,000m² elementary school designed to accommodate 840 students and staff. Total project cost was US $28,026,925, excluding land. As stated by the architects in their AIA COTE Top 10 Design Awards application, daylighting all school spaces was a primary design objective. The building is organized around three-story wings along a central circulation and shared spaces area 2.19, 2.20. Each wing has six classrooms – three facing south and three facing north; and all classrooms have sloping ceilings allowing for improved daylight distribution. The south facing classrooms employ the LightLouver™ 2.21-2.23 daylighting system to collect and redirect daylighting deep into the classroom, while eliminating all glare and direct sunlight. Horizontal lightshelves above the "vision windows" provide additional solar control. Daylighting strategy allows lights to be off during 43% of daylight hours.

Interior and exterior installed lighting power falls 38% and 54%, respectively below ASHRAE 90.1 energy standard requirements. Daylighting and efficient lighting systems account for 41% of the savings in the connected interior lighting power. Energy modeling revealed cooling, ventilation, and lighting to be the largest baseline energy loads. Overall, the building is expected to consume 52.7% less energy than the baseline design and meet the 2030 Challenge.

Daylighting was an important design prerequisite at the San Francisco Public Utilities Commission (SFPUC) LEED Platinum rated Building 2.24. It is a 27,750m², 13-story Class-A office building, designed by a joint venture of two local firms – KMD Architects and Stevens & Associates, to achieve long-term cost savings to the city of San Francisco. The building was completed in June 2012. The SFPUC building is wrapped in a double-glazed, high-performance curtain wall with operable windows. It has interior and exterior shading devices for controlling glare, increasing daylight, and minimizing heat gain. One of the main design considerations was the impact that the building would have on human performance. Along with creating a world-class sustainable building, the designers constantly had the employees in mind in creating the healthiest, most effective and comfortable work environment (American Institute of Architects, 2013). Energy efficiency and excellent quality of light were two defining goals. Fixed lightshelves help bring natural lighting further into the work spaces without obstructing the views, while intricate sensors monitor glare and heat gain and control interior shades and exterior venetian blinds 2.25, 2.26. Movable windows are also located in these areas. These daylighting strategies allow the building to have the electric lights off 60% of the time and the building to consume 45% less electric lighting energy compared to office buildings of similar class.

The Advanced Micro Devices (AMD) complex was designed by Graeber, Simmons & Cowan of Austin, TX, and occupied in 2008. The buildings were designed and oriented to reduce the solar heat load, while preserving access to spectacular views, with maximum daylighting 2.27. The complex is totally powered using clean renewable energy with passive solar heating. Interior light-shelves with exterior shading devices in the form of fins were custom designed to bounce light upward through clerestory windows above, extending daylight deeper into the buildings' interiors 2.28. According to the Center for Maximum Potential Building Systems Report (Vittori and Fitch, 2008), the total energy savings of the LEED Gold certified AMD's Lone Star Campus equal 19.9%, compared to a similar base-case building that does not incorporate similar energy savings strategies.

The energy and cost cutting benefits of daylighting have been illustrated by many other studies examining the benefits of lighting controls when used either as single approach or in aggregate with other strategies. One of the most significant cost saving potentials of daylighting is its potential to reduce peak demand, as peak demand usually coincides with the time when daylight is at its maximum potential. For example, a study by the Energy Center of Wisconsin estimated that 22% savings on annual lighting and HVAC operating costs were realized in a controlled experiment involving the use of daylighting. Demand charge savings, stemming mainly from reduced cooling loads, represented nearly 50% of the cost savings realized (Energy Center of Wisconsin, 2005). In 2008 Southern California Edison (SCE, 2008) produced a report on the "Office of the Future" which surveyed several studies that provided energy savings for daylighting, occupancy sensors, and personal controls in open offices; vacancy sensors in private offices; and occupancy sensors in corridors. According to the survey the overall range of savings was between 6% and 80%. A study by Lawrence Berkeley National Laboratories conducted a comprehensive analysis of lighting. It concluded that lighting controls on average capture significant energy savings between

2.24

2.24 – The San Francisco Public Utilities Commission Headquarters, USA, designed by KMD Architects and Stevens & Associates (Photo courtesy: David Hancock)

2.25 – South facade showing fixed exterior lightshelves to bounce daylighting deeper into the exterior of the building (Photo courtesy: David Hancock)

2.26 – The interior of the SFPUC Building, USA, showing the exterior lightshelves

2.27 – Exterior of the Advanced Micro Device Building Complex in Austin Texas, USA

2.28 – Interior lightshelf reflects light off the ceiling and deeper into the building interior (Photo courtesy: Aide Fitch)

1/3 and 1/4 of lighting electric energy, depending on the individual control strategy, and up to nearly 40% for buildings in which multiple controls strategies are used (Williams et al., 2011). While these results may have limited value from a predictive standpoint, viewed in aggregate, they build confidence that daylighting coupled with lighting control strategies can and do provide significant energy savings in commercial building applications. This finding has significant implications for energy policy.

Economic Benefits of Daylighting Beyond Energy Savings

The economic gains of daylighting often are expressed in terms of energy savings, but benefits related to worker productivity are substantial and may even dwarf the energy savings. According to the U.S. General Services Administration, the agency of the U.S. federal government that manages all U.S. federal buildings, over the 40-year economic life of an office building, the salary costs were about 92% of expenditures, while construction and maintenance costs represented only 2% and 6%, respectively. Investments made to improve a facility through better lighting, heating, and cooling systems can easily be offset by the productivity gains (Romm, 1994). In typical office buildings, energy costs average US $2.54/m^2 (2013 US dollars) while annual employee salaries and benefits cost US $1400/m^2. Realized productivity gains, even if small, can have major economic benefits beyond and above the energy savings. A 5% improvement in productivity could offset more than 40% of the entire construction, operating, and maintenance costs combined over the economic life of an office building according to the GSA study.

Statistics and studies like the GSA study have spurred interest in examining the causal relationship between the physical environment and work performance. Work performance, however, is not always easily quantifiable. Productivity can have different meanings and is measured differently depending on the type of work performed. The early studies of productivity concentrated largely on workers in factories where the outcome easily can be quantified and measured. Observations of silk weavers, linen weavers, and leather production workers are a few examples (Elton, 1920; Weston, 1922, and Stenzel, 1962). In these early studies, productivity was measured primarily by the quantity and quality of output. Later studies shifted the attention to office workers. Output may be a sufficient metric for clerical jobs, but

as the world economy is shifting more to service-based industry, one cannot use the old metrics of production in all cases. Old metrics cannot be used to evaluate many creative and professional jobs. Other such measurements as absenteeism and human costs are employed today. Workers' satisfaction with the physical attributes and various aspects of the work situation is recognized as an important consideration of performance (Djukic et al., 2010). Although a causal link between satisfaction and job performance in office settings is difficult to establish, a large body of research seems to point in the direction that office workers perceive their personal satisfaction with the work environment as closely related to their job performance (Sundstrom, 1980; Leblebici, 2012).

In 2003 the Center for Building Performance & Diagnostics (CBPD) at Carnegie Mellon University in collaboration with the Advanced Building Systems Integration Consortium (ABSI) conducted an extensive survey of existing case studies from around the world that link improved building environmental quality to life cycle cost-benefits. They claimed that a review of 1000 abstracts and 100 promising papers would lead to on average only one case study with statistically significant data. The CBPD and ABSI amassed around 140 case studies, with approximately 50 linking high performance components and systems to energy as well as other life cycle benefits. The CBPD team has identified 12 studies linking improved lighting design decisions with 0.7–23% gains in individual productivity. Four studies identify the contributions of higher lighting levels and daylight simulating fixtures to 0.7–2% improvement in individual productivity at a range of tasks (Loftness et al., 2003). Also, the CBPD has identified thirteen studies linking improved access to the natural environment with gains in productivity. Seven of these studies have identified 3–18% increases in individual productivity and 40% increases in sales (an organizational productivity measure) as a result of the introduction of daylight in the workplace. Six studies further indicate that the addition of operable windows for thermal comfort, natural ventilation, or simply access to the outdoors can impact productivity by 0.4–15%. The upper range of these productivity improvements, from 10–15% increased productivity, are achieved in mixed-mode buildings using natural and mechanical ventilation systems (Loftness et al., 2003).

The number of controlled experimental studies is much lacking to explore the relationship between the impact of the environment on productivity. There is, however, ample anecdotal evidence that links daylighting to better sales in mercantile buildings and to better performance in office settings. One of the first studies ever published about daylighting and sales was a *Wall Street Jour-*

nal article written by a Wal-Mart executive (Pierson, 1995). Wal-Mart built a prototype store in Lawrence, Kansas, in which skylights were incorporated to admit large amounts of daylight into the store throughout the building. According to the article, this particular store registered a noticeable increase in sales in the areas under the skylights compared with the same departments in other stores that relied exclusively on electric lighting.

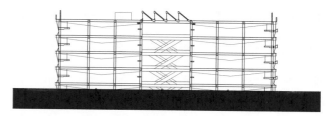

Another study cited extensively in the literature is the Lockheed Martin case. In 1983, Lockheed Martin Corporation moved 2,700 employees to a new 55,000m² facility, Building 157, that incorporated a large atrium, light-shelves, and other daylighting features 2.30, 2.31. Building 157 was designed by the firm of Leo A. Daly. The intent of the design architect was to use passive solar heating considering San Francisco's mild climate and low relative humidity where the building is located. The daylighting strategy, consisting of a tall ceiling, 60cm overhang from the south side of the building for shading, interior lightshelves from the north and south sides of the building

2.29 – Linear section of Lockheed Martin's Building 157, USA
2.30 – Exterior facade of Lockheed Martin's Building 157, USA (Photo courtesy: Russ Underwood)
2.31 – Linear atrium inside Lockheed Martin's Building 157, USA (Photo courtesy: Russ Underwood)

2.29, and a linear atrium covered with a sawtooth system facing north bring in deep daylight while minimizing glare and solar discomfort. After the move, Lockheed Corporation registered an increase of 15% in workers' production. Interestingly absenteeism dropped by 15% (Thayer, 1995). Also, it is reported that Building 157 saves 50% in energy bills compared to a reference building that meets California energy code. The company saved US $500,000/year in energy bills within the first year of occupancy.

A story fairly similar to Lockheed Martin's story was reported by the study of the headquarters of International Netherlands Group (ING) in Amsterdam, the Netherlands. The building houses the country's second largest bank 2.32-2.34. This 54,000m² building is largely daylit and relies mostly on passive environmental controls systems. According to the Rocky Mountain Institute (2008), this building uses less than 1/10 of the energy of the previous ING headquarters building and 1/5 of the energy used by most similar conventional new office buildings in the Netherlands. The annual energy savings are approxi-mately US $2.9 million. Not only has the building been a tremendous success financially, but employee absenteeism has decreased substantially.

Pennsylvania Power & Light reported that after completing building upgrades to use more daylight, absenteeism rates dropped 25%, productivity increased 13.2%, and energy costs declined 69%. The original energy payback was calculated to be a 24% annual return on investment. Once the employee productivity and reduced absenteeism were factored in, however, the actual return on investment was approximately 1,000% per year. In other terms, it was estimated that the lighting retrofit paid for itself not in the 4.1 years esti-mated, but in just 69 days (Center for Energy & Climate Solutions, 2013).

It is clear from the above discussions and anecdotal evidence that the incentive for daylighting, measured in economic sense, goes beyond energy savings. Savings resulting from improvements in sales or in productivity are substantial and may far outweigh the energy savings.

2.32

2.33

2.32 – ING Bank Headquarters in Amsterdam, the Netherlands, allows plenty of possibilities for daylighting from all sides and from the rooftop of the building. (Photo: M. Boubekri)

2.33 – Interior of the ING Headquarters building in Amsterdam, the Netherlands (Photo: M. Boubekri)

2.34 – Conference room of the ING Headquarters building in Amsterdam, the Netherlands (Photo courtesy: Ron Kok, ING)

CHAPTER 3

DAYLIGHTING AND HEALTH

In 2008 I wrote a book discussing the topic of architecture, daylighting, and health (Boubekri, 2008). Most of the discussion in that book focused on two main aspects of health related to daylighting or lack thereof, which I will summarize briefly in this chapter. One of those health issues relates to vitamin D deficiency and illnesses resulting from it. The second health issue is people's diurnal circadian rhythm and related depression and how daylight may impact them. Moreover, I will discuss in this chapter some additional topics, namely, the restorative effect of nature in general and of windows and daylight in particular. I also will discuss sleep disorders as they pertain to our insufficient exposure to daylight, particularly at our places of work. My entire hypothesis in discussing health related benefits of daylighting, or illnesses when daylight is lacking in our lives, is based on two facts. First, it is generally agreed that most people in the U.S., and perhaps elsewhere, spend the majority of their lives indoors, some say up to 90%. If we believe or can substantiate the connection between light and health, as I believe it has been ascertained, then architecture has a vital role to play in our health. This role is even more crucial in the northern latitudes where, during the long and dark winter days, people go to work and return home when it is dark. The hours when daylight is plentiful, the majority of people are indoors at work or at school T 3.1.

Daylighting, Vitamin D, and Health

Vitamin D is produced in our bodies through photosynthesis. When skin is exposed to ultraviolet-B radiation (UV-B), vitamin D is produced. Vitamin D helps regulate the body's absorption and use of calcium and phosphorus, both vital for normal growth and the development of bones and teeth. It also stimulates intestinal absorption and re-absorption in the kidneys and helps to maintain calcium and phosphorus levels in blood. Vitamin D enables bones and teeth to harden by increasing the deposition of calcium and may also assist in the movement of calcium across body cell membranes.

Under normal living conditions with sufficient exposure to sunlight the skin can produce 80% to 100% of all our bodies' requirements for vitamin D (Glerup et al., 2001). Food is the second source of vitamin D in our bodies, but relatively it is produced in much smaller portions than what sunlight is capable of providing. Numerous studies that have examined specific types of populations that are not very mobile, (e.g., physically handicapped, hospital patients, or geriatric populations in nursing homes that rely on help to move around or to go outside) have shown that vitamin D levels in such populations are very low in winter. Such deficiencies usually are not overcome by diet alone (Inderjeeth et al., 2002; Webb et al., 1990; Landin-Wilhelmsen et al., 1995). Surprisingly, vitamin D deficiencies also were found among many women in some Middle-Eastern countries, who cover their entire bodies, including their faces and hands (Hobbs et al., 2009; Saadi et al., 2007). For these women, it is rare when their skin is in contact with the direct sun even though there is plentiful sunshine in such countries. The postmodern lifestyle has confined these women to live in air-conditioned homes that no longer contain the central open-air courtyard that used to be a typical feature of the old Arabian house and where the women could remove the veil in total privacy and expose their skin to sunlight. These studies also have proven that we cannot receive all vitamin D requirements from food alone. Food has not proven to be a palliative substitute for sunlight.

According to many studies, one of the most significant positive impacts of sunlight is the effect of vitamin D on the prevention of internal cancers (Gandini et al., 2011; Grant and Garland, 2006; Ma et al., 2011). Consistent negative correlations have been found between sunlight (UV-B radiation) and cancer mortalities due to internal cancers such as ovarian, breast, colon, among men and women, white and black [3.1-3.5]. In other words, in places where the sunlight is abundant, there are fewer incidences of mortality from internal cancer, and higher incidences are found in the northern latitudes where sunlight is scarce.

The impact of vitamin D deficiency can be observed in many at risk population groups. Many bedridden hospital patients who stay in a hospital more than a month and who are not very mobile become vitamin D deficient, as patients do in intensive care units (ICU). Higgins et al. (2012) concluded in a study that low levels of vitamin D

T 3.1 – Length of days (DL) at various latitudes on the 21st of each month and amount of daylight hours (DH) before and after 8AM–5PM work hours

T 3.1

	35°N. lat. (Los Angeles, USA)		40°N. lat. (New York, USA)		45°N. lat. (Turin, Italy)		50 N. lat. (Vancouver, Canada)		55 N. lat. Copenhagen, Denmark)		65 N. lat. (Reykjavik, Iceland)	
	D.L.	D.H.	D.L.	D.H.	D.L.	D.H.	D.L.	D.H.	D.L.	D.H.	D.L.	D.H.
Jan. 21	10hrs 2mn	2hrs 2mn	9hrs 38mn	1hr 38mn	9hrs 11mn	1hr 11mn	8hrs 36mn	36mn	7hrs 52mn	-8mn	5hrs 14mn	-2hrs 46mn
Feb. 21	11hrs 1mn	3hrs 1mn	10hrs 50mn	2hrs 50mn	10hrs 35mn	2hrs 35mn	10hrs 19mn	2hrs 19mn	9hrs 58mn	1hr 58mn	9hrs 7mn	1hr 7mn
Mar. 21	12hrs 4mn	4hrs 4mn	12hrs 4mn	4hrs 4mn	12hrs 4mn	4hrs 4mn	12hrs 4mn	4hrs 4mn	12hrs 4mn	4hrs 4mn	12hrs 4mn	4hrs 4mn
Apr. 21	13hrs 8mn	5hrs 8mn	13hrs 22mn	5hrs 22mn	13hrs 38mn	5hrs 38mn	13hrs 58mn	5hrs 58mn	14hrs 21mn	6hrs 21mn	15hrs 35mn	7hrs 35mn
May 21	14hrs	6hrs	14hrs 24mn	6hrs 24mn	14hrs 54mn	6hrs 54mn	15hrs 29mn	7hrs 29mn	16hrs 15mn	8hrs 15mn	19hrs	11hrs
June 21	14hrs 22 mn	6hrs 22mn	14hrs 50mn	6hrs 50mn	15hrs 24mn	7hrs 24mn	16hrs 6mn	8hrs 6mn	17hrs 6mn	9hrs 6mn	21hrs 7mn	13hrs 7mn
July 21	14hrs	6hrs	14hrs 25mn	6hrs 25mn	14hrs 58mn	6hrs 58mn	15hrs 29mn	7hrs 29mn	16hrs 16mn	8hrs 16mn	19hrs 2mn	11hrs 2mn
Aug. 21	13hrs 4mn	5hrs 4mn	13hrs 22mn	5hrs 22mn	13hrs 38mn	5hrs 38mn	13hrs 38mn	5hrs 38mn	14hrs 20mn	6hrs 20mn	15hrs 35mn	7hrs 35mn
Sept. 21	12hrs 4mn	4hrs 4mn	12hrs 4mn	4hrs 4mn	12hrs 4mn	4hrs 4mn	12hrs 4mn	4hrs 4mn	12hrs 4mn	4hrs 4mn	12hrs 4mn	4hrs 4mn
Oct. 21	11hrs	3hrs	10hrs 46mn	2hrs 46mn	10hrs 32mn	2hrs 32mn	10hrs 15mn	2hrs 15mn	9hrs 57mn	1hr 57mn	8hrs 49mn	1hrs 49mn
Nov. 21	10hrs 2mn	2hrs 2mn	9hrs 38mn	1hr 38mn	9hrs 9mn	1hr 9mn	8hrs 43mn	2hrs 43mn	8hrs 11mn	11mn	5hrs 10mn	-2hrs 50mn
Dec. 21	9hrs 38mn	1hr 38mn	9hrs 4mn	1hrs 4mn	8hrs 34mn	0hr 34mn	7hrs 51mn	-9mn	6hrs 53mn	-1hr 07mn	2hrs 52mn	-5hrs 8mn

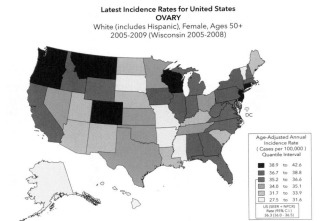

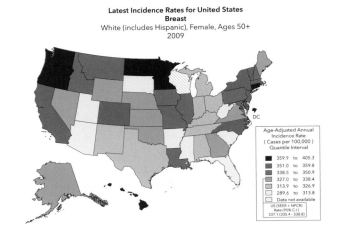

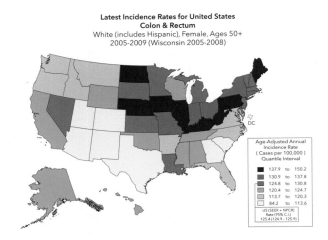

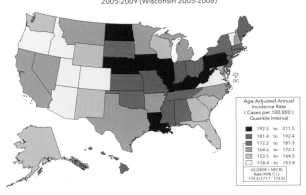

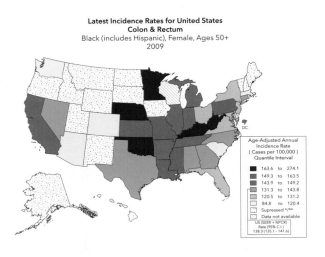

3.1 – Map showing the latitudinal distribution of ovarian cancer incidence rates among white females ages 50+ between 2005 and 2009 in the United States (Source: National Cancer Institute)

3.2 – Map showing the latitudinal distribution of breast cancer incidence rates among white females ages 50+ between 2005 and 2009 in the United States (Source: National Cancer Institute)

3.3 – Map showing the latitudinal distribution of colon and rectal cancer incidence rates among white females ages 50+ between 2005 and 2009 in the United States (Source: National Cancer Institute)

3.4 – Map showing the latitudinal distribution of colon and rectal cancer incidence rates among white males ages 50+ between 2005 and 2009 in the United States (Source: National Cancer Institute)

3.5 – Map showing the relationship between breast cancer mortality rates among white females of all ages between 1970 and 1994 and latitude in the United States (Source: National Cancer Institute)

3.6 – Distribution of SAD occurrence in the United States (Source: National Institute of Mental Health)

are associated with longer time to ICU discharge alive and a trend toward increased risk of ICU-acquired infection. Other population groups who are either vitamin D deficient or at risk of becoming vitamin D deficient are elderly persons whose mobility depends on care providers, workers in windowless environments, and people living or working in highly dense areas with limited access to sunlight in their streets and homes.

Daylight and Seasonal Affective Disorder

Physiologically, our bodies need high intensities of light to regulate and entrain our daily circadian cycle. High intensity of light, usually found abundantly in daylight, and especially in sunlight, serves as a major facilitator for the secretion of the serotonin hormone. Serotonin is responsible for our state of alertness. When high levels of light pass through the eye, impulses are sent to the visual cortex in the brain and other parts of the brain related to our emotions and hormonal functions. Starting from the eye, the circadian rhythm begins and continues through the retinal-hypothalamic channel to the brain. The hypothalamus is part of the human endocrine system

that orchestrates all chemical and physical processes of our metabolism and all the chemical reactions in each of the cells of our body. It is responsible for a number of such processes as energy and fluid balance, growth and maturation, circulation and breathing, emotional balance, reproduction, heat regulation, and activity and sleep patterns. The sleep-wake cycle is the most obvious example of the multiple variations in hormonal rhythms that happen over a 24-hour period. At low light levels, melatonin secretion increases, and the signs of drowsiness or sleepiness occur (Boyce, 2003; Boyce and Kennaway, 1987). During the dark phase of the 24-hour light-dark cycle, the pineal gland synthesizes the hormone melatonin, which is then circulated throughout the body by the bloodstream. At high light levels, melatonin is suppressed and serotonin is secreted. When melatonin levels increase, serotonin levels usually decrease since serotonin is being replaced by melatonin. When these normal cycles are disrupted either by insufficient exposure to light as in building interiors or for other reasons, melatonin or serotonin may be suppressed. These disruptions may be due to poor architectural design, but may have to do with other reasons beyond architecture. For example, a study found that exposure to light from self-luminous displays may be linked to increased risk for sleep disorders because these devices emit optical radiation at short wavelengths, close to the peak sensitivity of melatonin suppression (Wood et al., 2013).

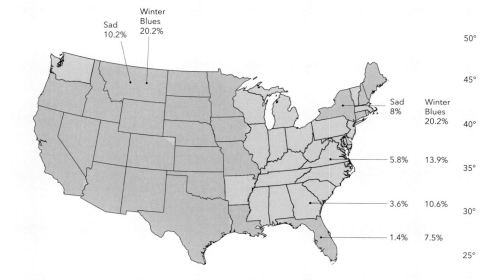

3.6

3.7 – Bright daylight deflected by exterior prism louvers and highly reflective curved aluminium ceiling panels of the Sparkasse Fürstenfeldbruck building, Germany, can make SAD less acute for the building occupants (Photo courtesy: Bartenbach GmbH).

3.8 – A windowless work environment can reduce the number of daylight hours workers are exposed to.

3.9 – Use of bright-light therapy as an antidote to Seasonal Affective Disorder

The seasonal depression phenomenon, often found among people living in northern latitudes 3.6 and typically referred to as Seasonal Affective Disorder or SAD, is another commonly known effect of light that is related to our endocrinal system. SAD is a form of depression usually associated with the short days and long nights of winter. SAD is due to an imbalance of brain chemicals (melatonin and serotonin) that leads to sleep and mood changes during part of the year. The symptoms of SAD typically tend to begin in the fall each year, lasting until spring. In winter seasonal affective disorder, the imbalance occurs due to too little sunlight. More than 10% of the population of Finland suffers from SAD. In Northern Europe, an estimated 12 million people suffer from Seasonal Affective Disorder. In the United States, about 4% to 6% of the population may have it, but 10% to 20% might have milder winter blues (Avery and Norden, 1998; Hellekson, 1989). The highest occurrence of SAD is found in the northernmost parts of the United States, between the 45 and 50 degrees north latitude. Most people with SAD are women whose illness typically begins in their twenties, although men also report SAD of similar severity and have increasingly sought treatment. SAD can also occur in children and adolescents (Magnusson and Partonen, 2005). The mean age of onset usually occurs in the early twenties and women outnumber men by a ratio of 4 to 1. Melatonin levels in those experiencing SAD are higher than normal during the day, so sufferers experience sleepiness, fatigue, and other melatonin-induced effects. They also are prone to serotonin deficiency symptoms such as negative emotional states and poor performance.

Treatment options are available to help ease the symptoms of Seasonal Affective Disorder and to return the affected person to a state of seasonal enjoyment. Spending time outside may be enough to eliminate symptoms. Natural daylight will reduce symptoms in more severe cases of SAD. SAD sufferers should try to spend one to two hours outside, even on cold or cloudy days. A study conducted in Switzerland showed SAD sufferers who took a one-hour morning walk outdoors did better than those who used low-dose (2,800 lux) light therapy (Wirz-Justice, 2003). However, daylighting can help in making SAD less acute by making high-intensity levels of daylight available in certain parts of our workplaces 3.7. Making indoor rooms bright and sunny can certainly provide some remedy. Arrange furniture to put desks and favorite chairs close to sunny windows. Even on gray overcast days, zenithal light is intense enough for several hours during the day to ensure levels above 1000 lux which are the minimum recommended levels for SAD treatment (Pail et al., 2011).

The symptoms of SAD are extreme fatigue and lack of energy, greater need for sleep, cravings for carbohydrates, which can often lead to weight gain, depression, and low morale and sadness, irritability, anxiety, loss of libido, menstrual difficulties for women, and possibly health problems. Several studies suggest that both natural and artificial bright light can significantly improve SAD. Research has established a direct correlation between the degree of vulnerability to SAD and exposure to natural light. It is widely held that higher levels of melatonin caused by fewer hours of daylight contribute to SAD. Fewer hours of daylight may be caused by latitudinal and seasonal factors or by architectural conditions such as people working in windowless spaces 3.8. Patients suffering from SAD report that their depression worsens whenever the sky is overcast at any time of the year and when their indoor lighting levels are decreased. SAD sufferers living in northern latitudes note that their winter depressions become more severe the farther north they live (Lam et al., 2001). Researchers now speculate that by using light as a therapeutic agent, 80% of SAD sufferers can be cured 3.9. Studies, as we have noted, also have found that the effectiveness of light therapy depends not only on the intensity of light but also on the duration of exposure and the spectral quality of the light. One can conclude that because of its numerous positive attributes, natural light is one of the best antidepressant agents available, one that is more efficient than electric light. It is almost impossible to combat depression by illuminating a building with light at levels of 2,500 lux or even 10,000 lux. Such illumination, however, can be achieved with natural light. On a sunny day, the illuminance outside can be as high as 100,000 lux and on a cloudy day it may reach 20,000 lux. What is interesting to point out to architects is that we spend the majority of our lifetime indoors because of weather and the necessities of work. It is, therefore, all the more important for architects to design buildings that provide therapeutic light levels, preferably with daylight. Buildings ought to be designed not only as places for shelter and to house necessary activities but also as places contributing to better mental and physical health.

Since light intensity is a catalyst for serotonin secretion, there is reason to believe that daylight deficiency may cause such disorders. Working in a windowless environment or in spaces that are deprived of adequate daylight may induce SAD. The natural balance between serotonin and melatonin levels must be maintained for our internal clock to function properly. The absence of such a balance causes problems for people. The light levels that are needed to spur the secretion of serotonin cannot be supplied by electric light due to energy considerations. Studies have shown that levels higher than 1,000 lux would be needed for such a reaction to occur. Most buildings are lit at levels averaging 500 lux or possibly less. Exposure to high light levels, which can be supplied

3.10

3.10 – Typical workstation of office workers without windows in Boubekri et al.'s study

3.11 – Typical workstation of office workers with windows and daylight in Boubekri et al.'s study

3.12 – Actograms of light exposure recorded using wrist actigraphy from a participant working in an office setting without windows (a) and a participant working in an office setting with windows (b) (Boubekri et al., 2013)

3.11

3.12

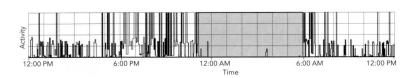

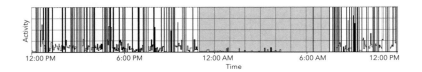

only by adequate daylighting, is necessary. Therefore one cannot deny the important role that architects and building professionals can play in this regard. In northern latitudes where winters are long and daylight hours are short, people go to work during the dark and return home during the dark. This is true for three to four months a year. In addition to people living in northern latitudes having short winter days and long winter seasons, there are plenty of people whose work conditions do not allow them to be in touch with daylight and may be considered at risk of experiencing SAD.

Depression, anxiety, and other forms of mental illness have become the greatest social problem in many countries, in the United Kingdom (UK) even surpassing unemployment. The economic cost in terms of lost productivity represents 1.5% of the UK gross domestic product, or around £17bn, or 1.5% of the UK gross domestic product (*The Guardian*, 2006). The National Health Service (NHS) in the UK has developed the largest mental health intervention program in history. The Improving Access to Psychological Treatments (IAPT) initiative mandates access to effective treatments for depression and other psychological problems. The argument behind this initiative is mostly economic. As recognized by many studies, depressed people are less likely to work, have more disability days, and are less likely to be able to contribute economically. Such an initiative is, therefore, a good investment and makes good economic sense (Leahy, 2010).

These health issues have economic consequences. In 1990, the economic burden of people with depression was estimated to be $52.9 billion considering the workplace costs attributable to days missed from work and loss of productivity, accounting for 60% of the economic burden (Greenberg, 2003; Marcus and Olfson, 2010). Depressed people lose 5.6 hours of productive work every week when they are depressed. Eighty percent of depressed people are impaired in their daily functioning (Pratt and Brody, 2008).

Daylight and Sleep Quality

There is much evidence that links insufficient sleep and/or reduced sleep quality to a range of significant short-term impairments such as memory loss, slower psychomotor reflexes, and diminished attention (Sigurdson and Ayas, 2007). If windowless environments affect office workers' sleep quality, there will be subsequent effects not only individually but also on a societal level, leading to more accidents, workplace errors, and decreased productivity. Sleep quality is also an important health indicator that has potent effects on mood (Leppämäki et al., 2003;

Bower et al., 2010), cognition performance, and health outcomes such as diabetes, cancer, depression, and other illnesses (Nebes et al., 2008; Knutson et al., 2006; Berger et al., 2006). Therefore, it is crucial to consider the effects of daylight as it may provide a profound way to improve workers' productivity and health as well as the safety of the community they work and live in.

Studies exploring the impact of daylight exposure, or lack thereof, on the health of office workers are very scarce. A recent study took on the task of exploring this relationship and set out to examine the influence of daylight in the workplace by the existence or absence of windows on office workers' sleep patterns, physical activity, and quality of life via actigraphy and subjective measures (Boubekri, 2014). Two groups of office workers were compared, namely, those with access to windows and daylight and those without windows, in terms of overall health and well-being, subjective sleep quality using well-validated scales, and objective measures of sleep and light exposure via actigraphy [3.10, 3.11].

Results from actigraphy confirm that workers with windows in the workplace had almost twice as much white light exposure during the workweek compared to workers without windows. The results of this study also demonstrate a strong association between workplace exposure to daylight and office workers' sleep quality, activity patterns, and quality of life. Workers in environments with windows not only had significantly more daylight exposure during the workday but also slept an average of 47 minutes more per night with a trend towards better sleep efficiency than those working in environments without windows. [3.12]

While sleep disturbance is often reported in our society for various reasons such as pressures in the workplace or at home or a habitual behavior, the relationship between lighting and sleep suggests that lighting during the daytime may also affect subsequent sleep duration and quality. Although sleep loss is often considered a harmless and efficient solution to the demands of modern society's schedules, research has shown insufficient sleep and reduced sleep quality have myriad negative health consequences. Among many consequences, partial sleep loss and poor sleep quality result in higher evening levels of the stress hormone cortisol (Sun Han et al., 2012) reduced thyroid-stimulating hormone (TSH) with altered thyroid axis function, impaired glucose levels that may increase risk of type 2 diabetes, and increases in appetite via decreased leptin satiety signals and increased ghrelin levels that stimulate appetite. Long-term patterns of daylight exposure at the work place may lead to long-lasting patterns of sleep and sleep quality that may subsequently contribute to numerous positive health outcomes.

Much literature also demonstrates insufficient sleep and reduced sleep quality may cause increased fatigue and deterioration of performance, alertness, and mental concentration which frequently lead to increased error rates and subsequent risk of injury. Therefore, workplace design with emphasis on daylight exposure to workers not only improves office workers' sleep quality and health, but may also contribute to their safety.

A most recent study found that just one week of abnormal, insufficient sleep can dramatically alter the activity of human genes according to a recent study published by the Proceedings of the National Academy of Sciences (Carla et al., 2013). For the first time ever, a direct relationship between sleep disorders and their effect on our genes has been established. The research, conducted at the University of Surrey, England, revealed that less than six hours of sleep a night has wide-ranging genetic implications affecting the activity of over 700 genes in our bodies. As a result, this study found that insufficient sleep affects the human blood transcriptome and metabolism but also disrupts circadian regulation and intensifies the effects of acute total sleep deprivation. One of the implications expressed in the conclusion of this publication is that if we cannot actually replenish and replace new cells, degenerative diseases can be expected. Through daylight deprivation, it is conceivable and quite possible that architecture may have a role to play in providing solutions to maximize human exposure to daylight and consequently reduce the potential for human health disorders.

Like many of these ailments, sleep disorders have economic costs. Medical errors also have been associated with sleep disorders. Long work hours and extended shifts among hospital workers are now known to contribute to the problem. Also there are public health consequences of sleep loss, night work, and sleep disorders, and they are not benign. Devastating human and environmental health disasters have been directly or partially attributed to sleep loss and night shift work-related performance failures. Some of the well-publicized tragedies include the tragedy at the chemical plant of Bhopal-India, the Three Mile Island nuclear reactor meltdowns, Chernobyl nuclear disaster in the Ukraine, and the Exxon *Valdez* oil spill. Not only have these disasters had a huge economic cost, but a significant impact on the environment and the health of communities as well.

Restorative Powers of Daylight and Views

Man by nature has been in tune with the natural environment ever since his arrival on earth. Daylight and views connect us with the outside world and inform us of where we are in place, season, and time within the daily cycle. Buildings mediate our exposure to the natural environment by providing shelter. That mediation may have positive or negative consequences for the building occupants depending on how that particular building is designed. Urban dwellers are not exposed to nature as much as suburban or rural dwellers and often take trips outside the city "to seek bliss" (Rudofsky, 1964) to be in contact with natural surroundings.

The lack of daylight or windows results in the absence of cues about the natural world which in itself is a form of sensory deprivation. The general understanding of sensory deprivation is the reduction or absence of usual external stimuli or perceptual opportunities, such as the outside world, commonly resulting in psychological distress or in such unpleasant psychological disorders as panic, mental confusion, depression, and other ailments. Sensory deprivation is recognized to be extremely detrimental to human beings. In extreme cases, sensory deprivation and isolation are used as a form of punishment in correctional facilities. A study compared workers in subterranean environments with workers in environments above ground with windows with a focus on the impact of reduced diurnal and seasonal variations and reduced sensory stimulation for persons working underground (Küller, 1996). The spaces below ground were perceived by the workers to be more enclosed, the lighting was considered to be less bright and less pleasant, and there were complaints of visual fatigue. The level of morning cortisol displayed a substantial annual variation in personnel above ground, whereas the annual variation below ground was much less pronounced. Also, the afternoon level of cortisol was lower for the personnel working in the subterranean environments.

Being exposed to the outside world and being in tune with the natural environment are believed to have positive influences on human beings. Gardens embellished with all their elements such as water, earth, plants, wind, and sun can nurture us with restorative energies and are believed to have restorative healing powers on sick people (Francis and Hester, 1995). The healing influences of a garden and what makes a garden a healing garden is today the realm of research in landscape architecture, environmental psychology, medicine, and horticulture. However, there is no scientific explanation that would be accepted by medical research as to the causal relationships and physiological inner workings to evidence this phenomenon. Protagonists of the healing powers of gardens do not suggest that gardens should replace medical interventions and be an alternative to medicine (Gerlach-Spriggs, 1998). There is, however, a body of evidence that points to the fact that gardens can aid the healing process, if only for psychological reasons and the sense of well-being engendered in their users.

The healing power of daylighting and views through windows may well fall into the realm of the healing powers of nature, much like gardens. Daylight, experienced through openings in a building, puts us in contact with the natural environment and the outside world, and gives us a frame of reference in terms of where we are in place and in time. The healing psychological power of the mere experience of daylight by a building occupant is an area that still deserves much attention and research. There is, however, a significant body of research that examined the question of whether the health benefits due to daylight and views of nature are real or not. Healthcare practitioners have known through history that persons recovering from illness recover faster in environments that have plentiful daylight. Florence Nightingale, the well-known aristocratic British nurse, was an advocate for maximizing natural light and sunlight in people's homes and in hospital wards. She noted that patients on the sunny side of wards had higher spirits and were more cheerful than those in areas that were not exposed to sunlight. The Lady with the Lamp, as she was known, went on to suggest architectural plans for hospital wards that are shallow so that they would receive sunlight from two sides instead of one. Sensory deprivation of the outside environment by hospital patients is an impediment to patients' recovery and has been found to be detrimental to patients' health and recovery speed (Wayne and Ronald, 2004; Schweitzer et al., 2004). Sick people in hospitals seem to improve faster when the exterior views through windows are of natural scenery and green landscapes (Ulrich, 1984). Ulrich's well-known study that spanned a nine-year period examined the restorative effects of views of natural landscape and gardens on surgery patients. Twenty-three patients assigned randomly to rooms with windows looking out on a natural scene had much shorter postoperative hospital stays, received fewer negative evaluative comments by their nurses, and took fewer analgesics than did 23 similar patients assigned to rooms with windows facing a brick wall.

Other studies of intensive care units suggested that the absence of windows may hinder or slow down the healing process of patients in hospitals. Higher levels of anxiety, depression, and delirium were observed among hospital patients who did not have any windows compared to those patients with windows. Healthcare facility

3.13 – Thunder Bay Regional Health Sciences Center in Ontario, Canada (Photo courtesy: Salter Pilon Architecture Inc.)

designers are now becoming aware of the healing powers of nature. Traditionally the emphasis in healthcare facility design has been on functional efficiency, costs, and providing effective platforms for medical treatments and technology (Ulrich et al., 1991; Horsburgh, 1995). The paradigm is shifting today towards devoting a lot of precious acreage for gardens and including such evidence-based design because it can make measurable differences in patients' health and hospital stays in North America and around the world.

Prominent examples include Thunder Bay Regional Health Sciences Center in Ontario, Canada 3.13. This award winning project was completed by Salter Farrow Pilon Architects Inc. The building was designed to use wood as a major structural element within the main atrium space 3.14. It was one of the first healthcare facilities in the Province of Ontario to use passive solar energy. Significant emphasis was given to daylighting in this hospital. The main public circulation corridor was gently curved to follow the path of the sun 3.15. This resulted in natural light bathing the public areas and opened the building to the outside healing gardens, terraces, and rehabilitation path system. Other innovations incorporated into the design include bringing daylight into the

heart of the nursing stations for the benefit of the staff and patients. It was the first hospital in Canada to bring daylight into the cancer radiation bunkers with the use of skylights within the treatment bunker itself 3.16. While technically challenging in the control of radiation, the impact on the psychological well-being of the patients has been enormous (Salterpilon.com, 2013).

The Nanaimo Regional General Hospital Emergency Department and Psychiatric Emergency Services Additions to the Nanaimo General Hospital in British Columbia, Canada, is another example where daylighting took a central role in the planning of the building layout. Designed by Stantec Architecture Ltd., this new wing of the hospital has been configured for functionality, indoor environmental quality, and sustainability. The addition's primary design goal is to reduce caregiver and patient stress by providing daylight and views of nature in all public and clinical areas. Each of the five patient care zones focuses on a plan-enclosed landscaped courtyard, bringing beauty, calm, and life-world connection to these high-stress environments 3.17. Operable glazed walls in the psychiatric emergency and intensive care lounges fold open to courtyard gardens 3.18, 3.19. The remaining

3.14 – Wooden structure used in the Thunder Bay Regional Health Sciences Center (Photo courtesy: Salter Pilon Architecture Inc)

3.15 – The circular atrium allows sunlight inside the Thunder Bay Regional Health Sciences Center throughout the day (Photo courtesy: Salter Pilon Architecture Inc)

3.16 – Skylights brings daylight into the cancer treatment wings of the Thunder Bay Regional Health Sciences Center (Photo courtesy: Salter Pilon Architecture Inc)

3.17 – New addition (upper right corner of image) to the Nainamo General Hospital in British Columbia, Canada, showing interior courtyards that provide daylighting to patients and staff (Photo courtesy: Stantec Architecture Ltd. © Nanaimo Hospital)

3.18 – Floor plan showing the L-shaped staff courtyard that opens off the lower-level clinician offices, lounges, and education spaces and the three interior lightwells (Photo courtesy: © Stantec Architecture Ltd.)

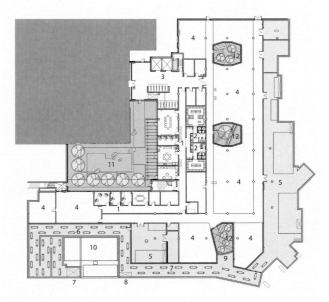

3.19 – One of the interior courtyards in the new addition of the Nainamo General Hospital (Photo courtesy: Stantec Architecture Ltd. © Artez Photography)

3.20 – The psychiatric emergency treatment courtyard that in good weather acts as an extension of the large patient treatment lounge in the new addition of the Nanaimo General Hospital (Photo courtesy: Stantec Architecture Ltd.; © Corey Stovin)

3.21 – First-floor plan and the landscaping of the Lucile Packard Children's Hospital, Palo Alto, California, USA (Rendering courtesy: Perkins & Will)

three upper-level courtyards extend down to the lower level, increasing daylight to future office-type functions. A staff respite courtyard lies in the gap between the existing hospital and the ED addition 3.20. The addition is set apart from the existing hospital to preserve existing building windows and to provide daylighting to staff work areas lining the inside of the L-shape on both floors. The hospital's four values underlie the addition's design principles: timely, respectful, quality care and a place people would want to come to work.

An important distinction can be made between conventional landscaping and a therapeutic garden explains Robin Guenther, FAIA, sustainable healthcare design leader at Perkins & Will. The design of Lucile Packard Children's Hospital in Palo Alto, California, by Perkins & Will, illustrates the emphasis on greenery as an integral part of the design of the hospital complex. A healing garden helps "connect to that primal biophilia," says Guenther (Melton, 2013). Just as important as gardens are to the recovery of patients, windows are now considered as an important therapeutic design ingredient and often are placed in specific locations so individuals

in waiting rooms can have access to a view. The Lucile Packard Children's Hospital is designed to be a hospital in a garden, connecting to site gardens and two roof terraces 3.21, 3.24. The interior environment brings the garden into the hospital with both ample views directly to the outside and materials, patterns, scale, and lighting inspired by garden environments. The site development creates four major garden spaces; collectively the development provides an additional 50,000m² of building and an additional 4.5 acres of habitat as compared to the existing site, demonstrating that sustainably designed buildings can serve human needs while also improving natural systems. The daylighting strategies for the hospital are framed by two primary requirements: maximize the healing powers of natural light while blocking the majority of direct solar gain as required by the innovative displacement ventilation system 3.22, 3.23. The displacement ventilation system is a key driver of the low energy design, however is more sensitive to solar gain than conventional systems, as direct radiant load from the sun projected on the floor can potentially create a thermal plume which can disrupt the displacement effect in other areas in the room.

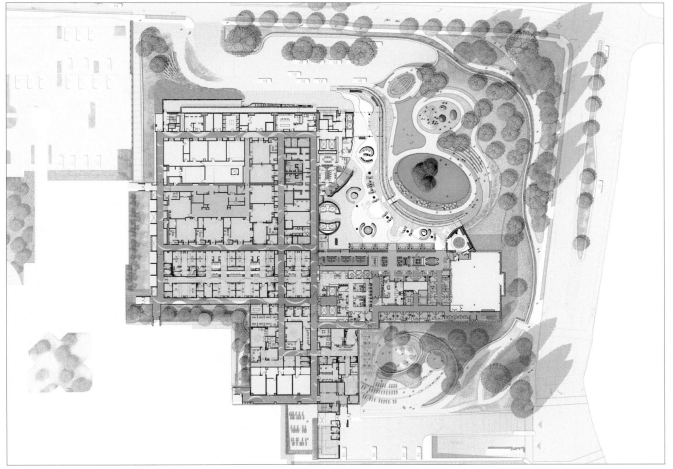

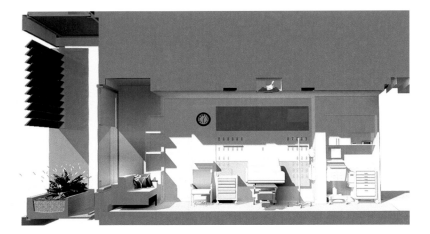

3.22 – 3-D section of patient room of the Lucile Packard Children's Hospital (Rendering courtesy: Perkins & Will)

3.23 – Patient room of the Lucile Packard Children's Hospital (Rendering courtesy: Perkins & Will)

3.24 – Emphasis on the exterior landscaping of the Lucile Packard Children's Hospital (Rendering courtesy: Perkins & Will)

The mere sight of sunlight seems to have therapeutic influences according to two Canadian studies that found sunny hospital wards to enhance healing compared to non-sunny ones. Patients with severe depression had shorter hospital stays if they had rooms with sunny views compared to those with non-sunny ones (Beauchemin and Hays, 1996; Walch et al., 2005). In a separate but follow-up study, the same authors found that patients with myocardial infarction staying in rooms with sunny views registered a lower mortality rate than their counterparts with non-sunny views (Beauchemin and Hays, 1998). Such emphasis on energy conservation as well as natural light is exemplified in the design of the three buildings on the campus of Indiana's Southeast Regional Treatment Center by the architectural firm HOK 3.13. The hospital design is based on sustainable principles to create an ideal healing environment. To enhance both energy efficiency and therapeutic benefits, interior spaces provide as much access to sunlight and views as possible. Corridors with relatively narrow floorplates surround a central courtyard to allow for maximum daylighting in patient rooms. Skylights, clerestories, and highly fenestrated hallways introduce natural light to public spaces. Shading devices and obscured glass in private areas prevent excessive glare 3.25-3.27.

Much like verdure and water, light seems to influence us in ways that we understand and in other ways that we do not yet understand. But this preference for nature seems to be a universal fact that transcends cultural norms and geographies. As Mirabel Osler, the prolific English writer and garden designer winner of the Sinclair Consumer Press Garden Writer of the Year Award in 1988 and the Journalist of the Year Award from the Garden Writers Guild in 2003, put it *"The spirituality of gardens has spanned the world, in time and geography. The mystical quality that a garden throws off is as powerful as the scent flowers."* (Osler, 1993).

3.25

3.27

3.25 – Exterior of the Southeast Regional Treatment Center, Madison, Indiana, USA (Photo: M. Boubekri)
3.26 – Sunlight controlled inside the Southeast Regional Treatment Center, Madison (Photo: M. Boubekri)
3.27 – Daylight inside the corridors of the Southeast Regional Treatment Center, Madison (Photo: M. Boubekri)

3.26

DAYLIGHTING METRICS

The amount of daylight that enters a building is dictated by the outside conditions and the building fenestration design. Today most of the daylighting calculations are performed with the help of computer programs that rely on weather prediction data accumulated over many years. Essentially, these computer programs are a series of mathematical algorithms developed by scientists that model the daylighting behavior of various daylighting systems. Whether the need is to estimate the energy savings from daylighting or to control the luminous quality resulting from a given fenestration design, it is necessary to calculate daylight levels inside a building. The changing character of daylight, however, adds complexity and difficulty in daylighting assessments of a building fenestration design and in standardization.

The temporal quality of daylight has made daylighting calculations and daylighting legislation a very difficult task. Unlike electric lighting standards which prescribe light levels to perform a given task (IESNA, 2000), illuminance based on daylighting standards do not exist anywhere in the world. The changing character of daylight would make such illuminance-based requirements nearly impossible unless such required daylight illuminance levels are associated to a time factor.

Static Daylight Modeling Metrics: The Daylight Factor Method

In order to eliminate the time factor in daylighting prediction, the *daylight factor* (DF) was developed in the early part of the 20th century. The DF is simply the ratio between the daylight illuminance level at a given point inside a room and the outdoor illuminance on the ground (Moon and Spencer, 1942). Under diffuse daylight conditions, which is what the DF method is limited to, the ratio between inside and outside illuminance remains constant. Consequently it is independent of time. The DF method is simple to use. The main reason for using a ratio was to avoid dealing with the variability of light outside. The DF method has been a metric primarily used by daylighting experts in litigation cases in the UK when expertise was required in court relating to the UK Prescription Act of 1832, known as the Ancient Light Doctrine which protected the right of an individual (or a window) to daylight for 20 years so that no neighboring structure could infringe on such right (Waldram, 1950).

The simplicity of the DF method made this metric the most prevalent one in countries that have any kind of daylighting recommendations in their building regulations. An example of DF legislation can be found in France, where the building code pertaining to educational buildings, *Le Cahier des Recommendations Techniques de Construction* of the *French Ministère de l'Education,* recommends a minimum DF of 1.5% in classrooms under overcast sky conditions (Ministère de l'Education, 1977). Similarly, in the United Kingdom (UK) during the post-war era, government regulation initially prescribed a minimum DF of 2% in classrooms. This regulation subsequently was dropped as it became apparent that it is not always possible to meet the 2% threshold from windows located on one side of the room only. Under such sky conditions, rooms needed to have either very high ceilings, side windows, and skylights, or side window from at least two sides to meet the 2% DF requirements.

DF is the most used metric when studying physical model experiments as well as among many practitioners (Nabil and Mardaljevic, 2005). The viability of many daylighting systems is based on the DF metric. DF is reasonably easy to calculate in real buildings or physical models with illumination meters. It is also used in many computer simulation programs as many of these computer models consider only the overcast sky condition in daylighting calculations 4.1.

While simple and widely used, the DF method raises concerns with its lack of consideration of any qualitative considerations and its limitations to overcast sky conditions (Reinhart et al., 2006). Some of the limitations of this method, for instance, are the same recommendations that would be given to all facade orientations since no consideration of seasonal variations, time variations, or differences in sky conditions are taken. The avoidance of sunlight as its inherent condition of applicability eliminates a very important element in architectural fenestration design. Depending on the geographical location and prevalent sky conditions, the DF method may or may not be suitable to assess a design solution from a daylighting standpoint.

Dynamic Daylight Modeling Metrics

Daylight prediction techniques are notoriously difficult. The problem is especially more complex when dealing with sunlight conditions. How does one evaluate this condition when the majority of available tools are geared towards dealing with the question of sufficient illumination almost exclusively? In 2000 I wrote a paper discussing some of the problems germane to daylighting legislation (Boubekri, 2000). Although there are many factors contributing to the quality of luminous environments, lighting design standards are almost entirely based on minimum illuminance requirements. Lighting standards generally prescribe minimum illuminance levels to be met in order for the observer to be capable of seeing or performing a certain visual activity. Lighting standards are well known for their inadequacy to deal with sunlight. Under such circumstances, light levels inside a room are much higher than any recommended minimum illuminance level for nearly any task. Quantitative and qualitative assessment models need to be pooled together in order to deal adequately with sunlight conditions.

In the last decade a series of dynamic daylight metrics have emerged. These computer-based simulation codes have appeared primarily because of the increased power of computing (Reinhart et al., 2006). Dynamic computing is based on a time series of illuminances within a room. The calculations span over the entire year, or a selected period, and are based on solar radiation data at the location of the building. A couple of these dynamic simulation techniques are discussed herein:

Daylight autonomy (DA) allows the user to calculate the percentage of a given time frame when a minimum illuminance reference level on a workplane is met by daylight. The cumulative hour-by-hour calculation of DA is based on an illuminance threshold that is user defined for a period of a year or another time frame chosen by the user.

4.1

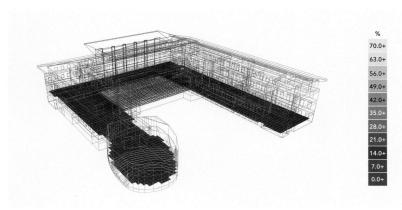

%
70.0+
63.0+
56.0+
49.0+
42.0+
35.0+
28.0+
21.0+
14.0+
7.0+
0.0+

4.1 – Daylight factor distribution of the Business Instructional Facility building at the University of Illinois at Urbana-Champaign (UIUC) in Illinois, USA, generated by the computer program Ecotect®

The DA varies in an inverse manner according to the threshold illuminance level selected 4.2. As the illuminance threshold increases, the DA is expected to decrease. This model was proposed by the *Association Suisse des Electriciens* (Association Suisse, 1989) and was improved by Reinhart and Walkenhorst. This new paradigm of dynamic daylight simulation was an important advance in the area of daylighting simulation since it considers the specific weather information of the geographic location of the project under all sky conditions. DA method permits the user to easily determine the potential electric lighting energy savings by calculating the percentage of time the user can rely on daylighting given a specified illuminance threshold. Generally speaking, this illuminance threshold is the ambient illuminance level that is found throughout the space. However, the user has the choice of selecting the illuminance threshold based on which DA is calculated. For example, in figure 4.2 the selected illuminance threshold of 400 lux (DA400) leads to a DA in the atrium

of the Business Instructional Facility building (BIF) on the campus of the University of Illinois at Urbana-Champaign of 100% between January 1 and December 31 from 8:00 AM to 5:00 PM.

Useful Daylight Illuminance (UDI) proposed by Nabil and Mardaljevic (Reinhart and Walkenhorst, 2001; Nabil and Mardaljavic, 2006) is a variation of the DA. It is a calculation of the percentage of time the interior daylight illuminance in an entire room falls within a range between 100 lux and 2000 lux. As the name suggests, this method considers illuminance levels below 100 lux of not much use to merit consideration 4.3, and those illuminance levels above 2000 lux as too excessive, possibly leading to visual or thermal discomfort as shown in 4.4, for instance. The assumption is that above 2000 lux there is a good chance that the room occupant would alter the condition of the room by some means such as pulling down shades.

4.2

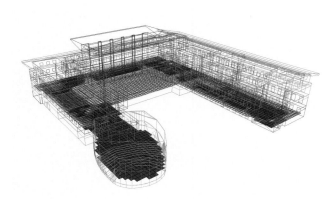

4.2 – Daylight autonomy graphics of the Business Instructional Facility building at UIUC, generated by the computer program Ecotect®

4.3 – The hours of very low illuminance levels inside the room would be excluded from the UDI.

4.4 – The hours of excessive illuminance due to excessive sunlight inside the room would be excluded from the UDI.

4.5 – East Wing of the National Gallery of Art in Washington, USA, by I.M. Pei, on an overcast day (Photo: M. Boubekri)

4.6 – East Wing of the National Gallery of Art by I.M. Pei, on a sunny day (Photo: M. Boubekri)

4.7 – British Museum courtyard, London, UK, under an overcast sky (Photo: M. Boubekri)

4.8 – British Museum courtyard under sunny conditions (Photo: M. Boubekri)

4.3

4.4

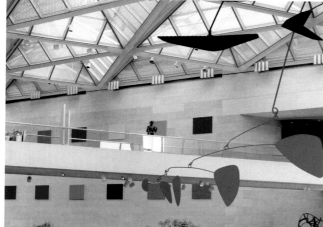

Behavioral Metrics of Daylighting

The UDI was the first approach to give some consideration to visual comfort considerations in daylighting modeling. However, when sunlight penetrates a room, much about that luminous condition remains unexplored. The temporal quality of daylight, be it diffuse or direct, evokes unique feelings and emotions, and a psychological reaction that cannot be measured with any calculation methods available today. The varying character of daylight gives an architectural space a dynamic quality not easily achievable with static electric lighting installations. The changing character of the atrium of the East Wing of the National Gallery of Art designed by I.M. Pei 4.5, 4.6, or the courtyard of the British Museum designed by Norman Foster 4.7, 4.8 are good illustrations of how spaces look and feel different under overcast and sunny conditions.

The soft diffuse daylight from an overcast sky filtered through the glass top cover falling on the grey colored walls of the atrium of the East Wing of the National Gallery of Art or of the British Museum conjures a feeling of openness and stillness. On a sunny day the contrasting shadows of the structural members of the roof cover and the bright sun spots evoke excitement and energy when sunlight is not too excessive and uncomfortable.

Lighting standards for the most part have been concerned with quantitative aspects of illumination, such as recommending minimum illumination levels for optimal task performance. When sunlight enters a space, illuminance levels generally are much too high for those standards to have any utility. In this case the quantitative information contained in these standards is irrelevant to the designer. Rather, the qualitative aspect such as glare and other factors the user might experience become more relevant and more useful to know.

Daylighting studies historically have used the overcast sky as the standard sky. The bulk of the first daylighting field originated mostly in the Scandinavian and northern European countries in the late 19th and early part of the 20th centuries. In these countries, the most prevalent sky condition is the overcast sky. The overcast sky is also the least favorable condition in terms of quantity of illumination available. The combination of these two reasons has made the overcast sky the default design in daylighting studies. The few design guidelines related to sunlight merely require avoiding thermal or visual discomfort.

Over the last two decades the focus on renewable energy sources to heat and illuminate our buildings has pushed the architectural practice and research communities to embrace sunlight as a source of energy and illumination that should be integrated in the design of all building types. Over the last century or so, we also have seen mounting evidence of a close relationship between the various aspects of the physical environment such as indoor air quality, lighting conditions, acoustical quality, and workers' performance, well-being, and health. Many post-occupancy surveys have put the lighting condition as one of the most important attributes for office workers. For all these reasons it became important to study daylighting including sunlighting conditions.

Sunlight often is considered an amenity for living or working spaces. However, the appreciation of sunlight by occupants depends on the type of building and the types of activities that take place in a space. People like sunlight, provided that no associated discomfort disturbs their activities; when sunlight enters a space, it creates a condition noticeable by the building occupant and may be perceived positively or negatively. Sunlight can cause a tremendous amount of visual discomfort and glare; it also can engender very positive sensations. From a purely visual outlook, small amounts of sunlight inside a space may be viewed as cheerful and warm. In this case, sunlight presence is a positive signal 4.9; sunlight may be viewed also as a visual distraction when it is excessive 4.8. Currently available lighting metrics are not designed to deal with such situations.

In the 1960s and 1970s, a few studies were conducted that explored the issue of sunlighting in buildings. Surveys were conducted primarily in the United Kingdom asking how many hours of sunlight residents would have preferred to have in their homes (Ne'eman et al., 1976; Ne'eman et al., 1976). The appreciation of sunlight depends, however, on the type of building and the types of activities that take place in given rooms; universal recommendations of sunlight penetration may not be feasible (Ne'eman, 1977). The metric of sunlight recommendations in terms of hours of sunlight exposure said nothing about the visual condition inside the buildings.

User-oriented architectural research has been based primarily on surveys in *post-occupancy evaluations* (POE) to acquire information about the success or failure of a design and what users like or dislike POEs. POEs involve systematic evaluations of opinions about buildings in use, from the perspective of the users. Their goal is to assess the success or failure of a design solution by evaluating how well buildings match users' needs. POEs allow designers and researchers to accumulate knowledge so as to inform future design decisions and research databases. Often POEs also may identify ways to improve building design, performance, and fitness for purpose. The main argument in favor of POEs is that building users are all people with a vested interest in their building. These vested people include staff, managers, customers or clients, visitors, owners, design and maintenance teams. Although some of the information acquired through these POEs certainly has been very useful, designers are cautioned against using this method of inquiry exclusively when it comes to adopting a user-oriented architectural research approach. Indeed, research has shown that people are not very good at evaluating accurately their preferences or experiences because generally they are not cognitively aware of, and in tune with, their environmental working conditions until these conditions become really bad or uncomfortable. Under such circumstances, the building occupants react to alter the uncomfortable situation by lowering window blinds in case of daylighting, for example. Moreover, studies have shown that people are not very apt at cognitively attributing different degrees of either good or bad of whatever condition they are being asked to assess. Gender, age, years of experience, and professional position are factors that can influence people's assessments about their workplace.

Given the available quantitative metrics limitations to assess qualitative aspects of lighting, and especially when dealing with sunlight, a different type of metrics is warranted to deal with the qualitative aspect of daylighting beyond the simple issue of glare. Some have suggested a user-based behavioral approach in evaluating luminous conditions that cannot easily be evaluated with the conventional metrics. Veitch and Newsham argued that, from a behavioral point of view, room setting, room occupants, and activities taking place in the room are three important factors that determine desirable lighting quality (Veitch and Newsham, 1998). Subjective measures, including room occupants' perceptions, preferences, and performance, are important markers of daylighting quality. As discussed above, sunlight can increase the indoor lighting levels far beyond recommended levels for most visual tasks. We need to find other measures to deal with sunlight in a room. One of these measures is to assess room occupants' responses to the lighting stimulus

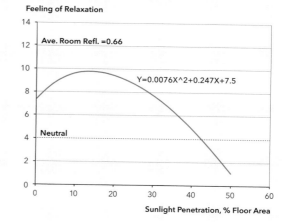

Feeling of Relaxation

Ave. Room Refl. =0.66

Y=0.0076X^2+0.247X+7.5

Neutral

Sunlight Penetration, % Floor Area

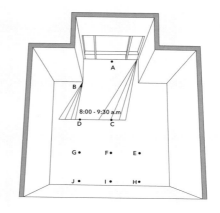

A

B

8:00 - 9:30 a.m

D   C

G•   F•   E•

J •   I •   H•

4.9 – Controlled and limited amount of sunlight penetration inside a corridor of the Meyerson Symphony Hall provides cheerfulness and a positive mood (Photo: M. Boubekri)

4.10 – Excessive sunlight penetration may be a distracting visual noise for a room occupant (Photo: M. Boubekri)

4.11 – Relationship between sunlight penetration as a percentage of floor area and emotional response for an office worker

4.12 – Experiment involving distance between room occupant and distance to the sun patch on the floor

through their moods and emotions evoked by the lighting environment. In lieu of the cognitive type of assessment used in post-occupancy evaluations, mood and affective assessment require the users to look inward and examine the way they feel about a particular environment. Room occupants' reaction to their environments can come in the form of mood changes, sometimes reflected by behavior. Measurement of mental processes that can be reported only by the person who is experiencing that mood is as important as behavioral outcome. Mood mediates environment and human behavior and influences the process that people use in solving problems and formulating judgments and evaluations (Yildirim et al., 2007; Iler, 2006).

In 1991, a novel paradigm and metric were proposed in consideration of sunlight in building interiors (Boubekri et al., 1991). This newly proposed metric of sunlight penetration used the percentage of the visible sizes of the sun patches inside a room in relation to the floor area of the room. Another novelty in this study was the use of occupants' mood and affective state as the occupants' response to sunlight penetration. Affective and mood responses were measured using Positive and Negative Affective Schedule (PANAS) used by the American Psychological Association (Watson et al., 1988). Ultimately the study revealed that despite people's preferences for and their liking of sunlight, only moderate amounts of sun penetration are desired inside their offices. An optimal sunlight penetration, between 15 and 25% of the floor area, was found to produce the highest levels of relaxation 4.11.

4.13 – Reflected glare or veiling reflection is caused by a reflection of incident light on a highly reflective surface (Photo: M. Boubekri)

4.14 – Disability glare reduces the ability to see anything (Photo: M. Boubekri)

4.15 – Direct glare caused by a very bright light source (Photo: M. Boubekri)

4.16 – Discomfort glare resulting from too much contrast between object and background (Photo: M. Boubekri)

4.17 – Discomfort glare caused by contrast between the bright window and its surroundings inside the BMW showroom in Munich, Germany (Photo: M. Boubekri)

4.18 – Representation of the source luminance L_s (a) and the background luminance L_b (b)

4.19 – Lateral displacement angle Ø (a) and vertical displacement angle θ (b)

A follow-up study examined whether the distance between a person sitting somewhere in a room and the sun patch on the floor 4.12 could be a factor that might influence the way a person feels about the room, reacts to the luminous condition, and consequently behaves (Wang and Boubekri, 2010). Distance to the sun patch, if found to be a significant variable, could have ramifications regarding fenestration design as well as office space layout. In this study, the relationship between distance to sun patch on the floor and room occupants' performance and mood response hypothesized as an inverted-bell shape relationship did not materialize.

While these behavioral studies provide useful insights and possibly new paradigms to evaluate the evidently complex luminous condition resulting from the presence of sunlight, it is important to calibrate whatever findings these behavioral studies may derive against a consort of cultural, geographical, and climatic influences that may be quite strong and may well be very different from the circumstances of the study in question.

Gender differences are also a major factor in the development of behavioral studies concerning lighting (Belcher and Kluczny, 1987; Putrevu, 2001; Yildrima et al., 2007). Behavioral differences of men and women are well documented in the literature of environmental psychology and other fields. Lighting studies have revealed the existence of marked differences between the way men and women perceive their luminous conditions or the way men and women are affected by lighting. Women tend to be more in tune with the characteristics of their workplace and are more critical of them than are men.

Visual Comfort and Glare from Windows

Where larger areas of fenestration exist within a building, the concerns about visual comfort are omnipresent. A daylighting strategy is an intentional and controlled use of natural light to accomplish a particular goal. With so much of the sky being exposed to a building occupant through windows, it is very important to control the amount of light that enters a building as well as the quality of the visual environment. A lack of attention to visual comfort issues often makes the best daylighting intentions ineffective. When glare from windows is not addressed during the design, occupants often introduce changes to ameliorate their visual comfort that negate the objectives of the daylighting solution. One of the main criteria of visual discomfort is glare. Glare interferes with visual perception caused by an uncomfortably bright

light source or reflection, a form of visual noise. There are different types of glare. Reflected glare, also known as veiling reflection, is a reflection of incident light that partially or totally obscures the details to be seen on a surface by reducing the contrast 4.13. Disability glare is experienced when an excessive amount of light enters the viewer's eye and impedes vision. Such is the case when a viewer looks directly at a very bright light source such as the sun. Disability glare reduces one's ability to perceive the visual information needed for a particular activity 4.14. Direct glare can be a bright sunlit surface inside or outside a building or an insufficiently shielded luminaire 4.15. In some ways direct glare is similar to disability glare, differing in the fact that vision is not completely hindered. Direct glare is caused by high luminances in the visual environment directly visible from a viewer's position.

Discomfort glare, on the other hand, is one of the most common problems in fenestration design and daylighting strategies. Discomfort glare is a type of glare which is distracting or uncomfortable and interferes with the perception of visual information required to satisfy biological needs but which does not significantly reduce the ability required for visual activities. Generally, discomfort glare is caused by too much contrast between a light source, or a window, and its surrounding background or an object and its background 4.16, 4.17. Some have suggested that glare has not received the required attention in contemporary architecture (Jakubiec, 2012).

There have been few metrics to assess and quantify discomfort glare. Researchers investigated glare from artificial light sources during the early and mid-1920s. The formula known as the *Cornell Formula*, a collaborative work between the Building Research Station in England, researchers from Cornell University in the United States, and experiments conducted by Chauvel and Dogniaux (1982) using actual windows, led to the development

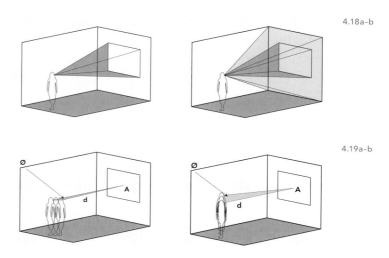

4.18a-b

4.19a-b

of the *daylight glare index* (DGI) in use for subsequent decades. Glare in this well-known glare formula is a function of the luminance of the source, its background luminance, the source size and location of the source, and the direction of viewing in relation to the window [4.18a-b, 4.19a-b]. The formula for the daylight glare index is expressed as:

$$DGI = 10 Log\, 0.478 \sum_{i=1}^{n} \frac{L_s^{1.6} \Omega^{0.8}}{L_b + 0.07\omega^{0.5} L_w}$$

Where:

L_s: average luminance of each glare source in the field of view (candela/m²) [4.13a]

L_b: average luminance of the background excluding the glare source (candela/m²) [4.13b]

L_w: average luminance of the window (cd/m²) (treated same as L_s)

ω: solid angle of the source seen from the point of observation (sr)

Ω: solid angle in steradians subtended by the source, modified for the effect of the position of the observer in relation to the source

n: number of glare sources.

Angles (ϕ) and (θ) represent horizontal and vertical displacement from normal line to the glare source as shown in [4.13]. The solid angle (ω) subtended by the glare source to the point of observation can be calculated as (Hopkinson, 1963; 1972):

$$\omega = \frac{hw\, cos\,\varphi\, cos\,\theta}{d^2}$$

In the DGI formula, Ω is the solid angle subtended by the window, modified by P_i, the position index of the window [T.4.1]. More information about the basis of P_i values modification can be found in Hopkinson (Hopkinson et al., 1966). It is given by the equation below:

$$\Omega = P_i \omega$$

Where:

P_i: position index of the window,

ω: solid angle of the source in steradians seen from the point of observation [T 4.1, T 4.2].

Zone	Acceptance level	DGI
Discomfort zone	Intolerable	>28
	Just tolerable	28
	Uncomfortable	26
	Just uncomfortable	24
Comfort zone	Acceptable	22
	Just acceptable	20
	Noticeable	18
	Just perceptible	16

Other researchers indicated that the formula is not directly applicable to a case where the window is parallel to the subject's line of sight. Dubois, in her study about the impact of shading devices on daylight quality in offices, referred to this issue by mentioning that the DGI should not be applied when discomfort glare is caused by non-uniform light sources like a window with venetian blinds, as an example. In the case of very large windows, some have found through experiments that the glare index value increased as the number of source subdivisions increased (Iwata and Tokura, 1998; Inkarojrit, 2005). Inoue and Itoh (1989) suggested that the DGI should be independent of background luminance when the glare source size becomes large, approaching 2π steradians. Under such a condition, the researchers suggest that the background luminance becomes highly influenced by the glare source itself. According to Aizlewood (2001), since the DGI is a daylight glare index and not a sunlight glare index, the DGI formula became unreliable when assessed with direct sunlight falling on the measuring apparatus. A study that examined the effect of window size and sunlight penetration on glare in a private office room found that the amount of sunlight penetration had no significant effect on sensitivity to glare for an observer facing the window or for a person sitting sideways to the sunlight source. For an observer sitting sideways, window size was not a factor in the perception of glare; glare was, on the other hand, significant for observers facing the window (Boubekri and Boyer, 1992).

T 4.1 - Glare acceptance levels and their related glare index
T 4.2 - Table of position index

Horizontal Angle (φ)

V/d	0°	6°	11°	17°	22°	27°	31°	35°	39°	42°	45°	50°	54°	58°	61°	63°	68°	72°	θ
1.9	-	-	-	-	-	-	-	-	-	0.02	0.02	0.02	0.02	0.02	0.02	0.02	0.02	0.02	62°
1.8	-	-	-	-	0.02	0.02	0.02	0.02	0.02	0.02	0.02	0.02	0.02	0.02	0.02	0.02	0.02	0.02	61°
1.6	0.03	0.03	0.03	0.03	0.03	0.03	0.03	0.03	0.03	0.03	0.03	0.03	0.03	0.03	0.03	0.03	0.02	0.02	58°
1.4	0.04	0.04	0.04	0.04	0.04	0.04	0.04	0.04	0.04	0.04	0.04	0.04	0.04	0.04	0.04	0.03	0.03	0.03	54°
1.2	0.05	0.05	0.06	0.06	0.06	0.06	0.06	0.06	0.06	0.06	0.06	0.05	0.05	0.05	0.05	0.04	0.04	0.04	50°
1	0.08	0.09	0.09	0.1	0.1	0.1	0.1	0.09	0.09	0.09	0.08	0.08	0.07	0.06	0.06	0.06	0.05	0.05	45°
0.9	0.11	0.11	0.12	0.13	0.13	0.12	0.12	0.12	0.12	0.11	0.1	0.09	0.08	0.07	0.07	0.06	0.06	0.05	42°
0.8	0.14	0.15	0.16	0.16	0.16	0.16	0.15	0.15	0.14	0.13	0.12	0.11	0.09	0.08	0.08	0.07	0.06	0.06	39°
0.7	0.19	0.2	0.22	0.21	0.21	0.21	0.2	0.18	0.17	0.16	0.14	0.12	0.11	0.1	0.09	0.08	0.07	0.07	35°
0.6	0.25	0.27	0.3	0.29	0.28	0.26	0.24	0.22	0.21	0.19	0.18	0.15	0.13	0.11	0.1	0.1	0.09	0.08	31°
0.5	0.35	0.37	0.39	0.38	0.36	0.34	0.31	0.28	0.25	0.23	0.21	0.18	0.15	0.14	0.12	0.11	0.1	0.09	27°
0.4	0.48	0.53	0.53	0.51	0.49	0.44	0.39	0.35	0.31	0.28	0.25	0.21	0.18	0.16	0.14	0.13	0.11	0.1	22°
0.3	0.67	0.73	0.73	0.69	0.64	0.57	0.49	0.44	0.38	0.34	0.31	0.25	0.21	0.19	0.16	0.15	0.13	0.12	17°
0.2	0.95	1.02	0.98	0.88	0.8	0.72	0.63	0.57	0.49	0.42	0.37	0.3	0.25	0.22	0.19	0.17	0.15	0.14	11°
0.1	1.3	1.36	1.24	1.12	1.01	0.88	0.79	0.68	0.62	0.53	0.46	0.37	0.31	0.26	0.23	0.2	0.17	0.16	6°
0	1.87	1.73	1.56	1.36	1.2	1.06	0.93	0.8	0.72	0.64	0.57	0.46	0.38	0.33	0.28	0.25	0.2	0.19	0°
	0	0.1	0.2	0.3	0.4	0.5	0.6	0.7	0.8	0.9	1	1.2	1.4	1.6	1.8	2	2.5	3	

Vertical displacement (V/d) — Vertical angle (θ) — Lateral displacement (L/d)

Other studies have suggested using vertical illuminance levels impinging on the observer's eye as an influential parameter in glare assessments (Aizlewood, 2001). In the same sense, Nazzal (2001) conducted an experiment using shielded and unshielded illuminance sensors to calculate DGI. His experiment was built on the hypothesis that the adaptation luminance has a significant influence. As a modification of the DGI, he suggested replacing the average luminance of each glare source in the field of view (L_s) in Chauvel's formula, with $L_{ext.}$, the average vertical unshielded illuminance from the surrounding environment (at the window). The DGI_N formula is expressed below:

$$DGI_N = 10 Log\, 0.478 \sum_{i=1}^{n} \frac{L_{ext}^{1.6}\, \Omega^{0.8}}{L_b + 0.07\omega^{0.5} L_s}$$

Despite the substantial progress in glare studies made during the last half of the 20th century, some questions remain unanswered by the DGI, particularly related to specific daylighting conditions. Does the quality of view influence Discomfort Glare? A study in Shieffield, United Kingdom, testing whether the quality of view influences glare discomfort found that Discomfort Glare lessened as the quality of the view became more inter-

esting to the viewers (Tuaycharoen and Tregenza, 2005; Yun et al., 2010; Kim et al., 2011). This study highlights the point that the perceived glare from windows, unlike glare from artificial sources, may be influenced by other aesthetic considerations. Generally, there have been two broad accounts of discomfort glare, one that considers glare response as being purely physiological caused by an element within the eye such as retina, muscle, or optic nerve to respond to the luminous condition. The second account regarding glare perception attributes glare to visual distraction which includes a degree of psychological effect as part of that perception. In this second account, the information content of the view is an important consideration albeit hard to measure. The quality of view may to a degree or up to a certain level compensate for some high glare levels.

CHAPTER 5

DAYLIGHTING PERFORMANCE OF SIDE-WALL WINDOWS

With the exception of a few building types, buildings are equipped with windows for daylighting, views, and ventilation. Today, buildings with entire glass facades are a common occurrence; yet, one cannot say that every building equipped with windows has adopted a daylighting strategy. The technical and perhaps widely accepted definition of daylighting refers to the "active" use and control of natural light to achieve a particular purpose, be it to save burning fossil energy or to improve building occupants' comfort and well-being or both.

Because most rooms in buildings are equipped with windows on a single side, it is important to address the daylighting performance of this type of design strategy and the tools available to designers to predict performance. Typical office buildings would have a floor to ceiling clearance of between 2.4 meters and 2.75 meters. With such a relatively low clearance, daylight illuminance levels drop precipitously as one moves away from the window wall. Experience has shown that the depth of the daylit zone along the peripheral walls where daylight can be considered of any use is only two or three meters deep 5.2. This situation is always seen as a major drawback of side-wall windows as viable daylighting strategies, particularly when the floor plate of a building is deep. Since most peripheral rooms in multi-story buildings have windows that provide daylight on only one side, electric lighting consequently is used most of the time throughout the space. With such typical ceiling heights and in order to be able to count on daylight for at least a portion of the day, a building width of no more than 20 meters is generally recommended. With a floor plate of 20 meters, 40% to 60% of the floor plate could be daylit for a good portion of the daytime hours while allowing for views to the exterior for most of the occupants 5.1.

Tall windows provide a much deeper daylight penetration; consequently deeper floor plates can be found as a result 5.3. Tall windows permit a better luminous quality inside the room by reducing contrast and glare and eliminating what is commonly called "the cave effect" caused by large disparities in light levels between the peripheral area near the windows and the building's central core.

To estimate the amount of daylight entering a building, a few daylight prediction methods are available to designers. Architects prefer simple design and prediction tools in the early stages of design. A simple equation found in North American and European design guides is a widely used daylight estimation tool (Enermodal Eng., 2002; Cofaigh et al., 1999; Din V 18599-4, 2005; US-DOE, 2005). It has been used and accepted despite its unknown

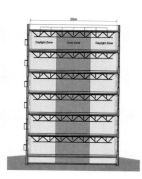

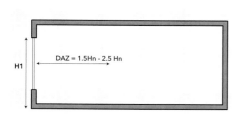

5.1 – Optimal depth of a build-ing for optimal daylighting

5.2 – Typical daylight distribution from a single side-window in a room with a typical ceiling height (Photo: M. Boubekri)

5.3 – Tall windows result in a deeper daylight penetration (Photo courtesy: Paul de Ruiter Architects)

5.4 – Depth of the "effective daylight zone" in the ubiquitous rule of thumb

origins. Some have referred to it as the "ubiquitous rule of thumb (URT) for window sizing" (Reinhart, 2005). In a very simple equation this URT relates the depth of the daylight penetration to the head height of the window (H_h) such that the depth of the "effective daylight zone" is equal to 1.5 H_h to 2.5H_h 5.4.

The "effective daylight zone" also has been labeled as the *daylight autonomy zone* (DAZ). The DAZ as a concept takes into consideration the changing characteristic of daylight and through computations suggests a depth or an area of the building where one can count on daylight for illuminating a given room. It is worth noting that the illuminance level in the DAZ concept is related to the type of activity taking place in the room. In an office building, for example, normally it would be from 8AM to 5PM and the target illuminance level may be different according to the needed light levels to achieve the visual activity taking place in the room (for example, 300 lux for an office or 500 lux for a classroom). Using such a metric, a Canadian study tested the validity of the URT through computer simulations (Reinhart, 2005) and found that over 85% of the daylit zone of a typical office room with a typical ceiling height falls within the wide range of 1.0 H_h to 2.5 H_h, as stated by the URT 5.5. As one increases or decreases the illuminance levels the depth of the DAZ change accordingly and in the same direction as the change in illuminance levels.

However, the conditions under which the URT applies are not clear, nor can they be found in the literature since the origin of this rule of thumb is really unknown. For example, we do not know the size of the window under which the URT is applicable. Also, we do not know if this rule of thumb is applicable under all sky conditions or whether it is limited to certain conditions.

While the URT takes into consideration only the height of the window as the only useful variable in predicting the DAZ, simple computer simulations tested its universal applicability and validity. The results of simple computer simulations using the Velux Daylight Visualiser© performed by students in a class exercise given by the author are illustrated in 5.6a-d, 5.7a-d, 5.8a-d. These figures indicate that both the depth and the breadth of the daylit zone are affected simultaneously by the height and the width of the window, not its height alone. The test room used in these simulations was an office that measured 8m by 10m with a ceiling height of 2.5m and a window stool of 0.9 meters. In 5.6a-d, the height of the window was kept constant at 1.20m above the window stool but the width of the window varied incrementally between 1m and 8m with 2m increments. Similarly, in 5.7a-d, the window height was kept at 1.60m above the same window stool and the window varied incrementally as in 5.6a-d. In 5.8a-d, the window width was kept constant at 3m but the window height above the window

5.5

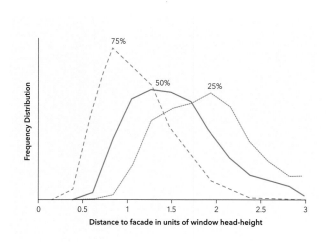

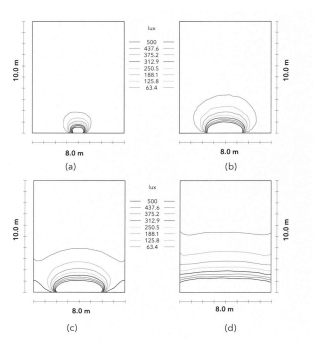

5.6

5.5 – Frequency distributions of predicted daylit zone depths with blinds for varying "cutoff" percentages of the maximum daylight autonomy in the space

5.6a-d – Daylight distribution for a 120cm-high south-facing window with 90cm sill on an overcast day at 12PM on March 21st in Chicago with an 800cm (width) x 1000cm (depth) x 250cm (h) room; **(a)** width = 100cm, **(b)** width = 300cm, **(c)** width = 500cm, **(d)** width = 800cm

stool was changed from 1m to 1.60m, with increments of 0.20m. As shown in these figures, the window height is not the only relevant variable in describing the extent of the daylight penetration. Moreover, these simulation results prove numerous facts, namely that: 1) the URT is not applicable when the window is small but may have some validity only when the width of the window is nearly equal to the width of the room; 2) both the window height and width are equally important in allowing daylight inside a room through a side wall-window.

The type of sky condition in a particular location controls the daylight levels available outside a building and consequently inside a room with a side-wall window. Although there are no really good climate metrics relevant to daylighting compared to those of heating degree-days or cooling degree-days used in thermal or energy simulation studies, it is important to consider the prevailing sky conditions when we examine the performance of windows on an annual basis. One of the metrics used is simply the probability occurrence of a clear sky versus an overcast sky condition. A study examined the effect of prevailing sky conditions in four different climates, the type of facade, the facade orientation and the ceiling clearance, on the daylight distribution from a curtain wall window (Arney et al., 2012). This study used another metric called the *useful daylight illuminance* (UDI) (Nabil

and Mardeljevic, 2005) to test how window design parameters affect daylight distribution. The UDI concept is a variance of the DAZ concept in that it calculates the percentage of time an illuminance array between 100 lux and 2,000 lux is achieved through the entire room in a given year. This illuminance range is explained by the assumption that illuminance levels below 100 lux are too low and too inconsequential to carry out most visual tasks, and illuminance levels above 2,000 lux are too excessive for adequate visual and thermal comfort. The four different climates considered in this study were based primarily on how they differed in their prevalent sky conditions: Dubai (clear: 73%, intermediate: 23%, overcast: 5%); London (clear: 16%, intermediate: 18%, overcast: 66%); Singapore (clear: 0.4%, intermediate: 15.1%, overcast: 84.5%), and Sydney (clear: 33%, intermediate: 34%, overcast: 33%). Figure 5.10 illustrates the variables included in this study and the conclusions are summarized in table 5.1.

The conclusions of this study show that the type of climate, window orientation, and ceiling height are factors having a significant effect on how a side-wall window performs. After the prevailing sky conditions, the room's ceiling height is the most significant factor. For example, an increase of 0.5m in the ceiling height could lead to a 30% increase in the UDI for a curtain wall window that extends from wall to wall. However, an increase in the

5.7

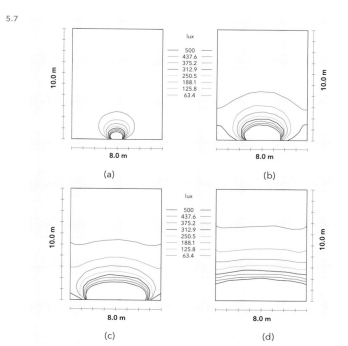

5.7a–d – Daylight distribution for a 160cm-high south-facing window with 90cm sill on an overcast day in Chicago in March at noontime with a 800cm (width) x 1000cm (depth) x 250cm (h) room; (a) width = 100cm, (b) width = 300cm, (c) width = 500cm, (d) width = 800cm

5.8

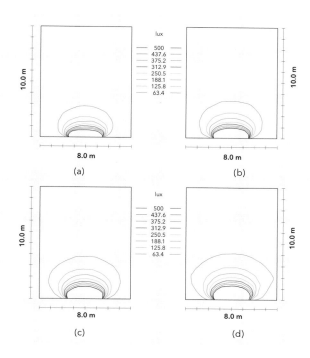

5.8a–d – Daylight distribution for a 300cm-wide south-facing window with 90cm window sill during an overcast day in Chicago in March at noontime with an 800cm (width) x 1000cm (depth) x 250cm (h) room; (a) height = 100cm, (b) height = 120cm, (c) height = 140cm, (d) height = 160cm

ceiling height results also in an increase in a room's volume to be heated or cooled, and trade-offs would have to be considered.

Most daylight prediction tools including the above discussed URT tend to ignore the context, a building's surroundings. Most of these tools assume a building with no buildings or other obstructions around. An urban setting, especially with dense, tall buildings, can lead to significant variations in the amount of daylight available outside a building or entering through a window. To that end, a series of computer simulations conducted by the author examined the impact of the urban density on daylighting performance. Urban density may be defined by several factors including building heights and street width. The location of the test room within a building, vis-à-vis the surrounding urban morphology, may be of significance as well. A parametric daylighting analysis using Ecotect® software tested the impact of building height, the street width, and the exterior surface reflectance of surrounding buildings on daylight levels inside a room within a building of three different shapes: rectilinear, L-shape and U-shape 5.10, 5.11, T 5.2. The particular test office room measured 4.50 meters x 9.0 meters with 2.50 meter floor to ceiling height, and windows that extend from wall to wall with a 0.9m high window stool. The daylight factor approach was used to assess performance. Daylight factor is the percentage of light at a given point inside a room compared to the external horizontal illuminance under diffuse daylight conditions.

The following are summaries of the results and the lessons learned from these simulations. It may be noteworthy to mention that in order to test for the effect of the exterior surface reflectance of an opposing building, we used 1% as the minimum reflectance, the lowest acceptable value by Ecotect®.

5.9

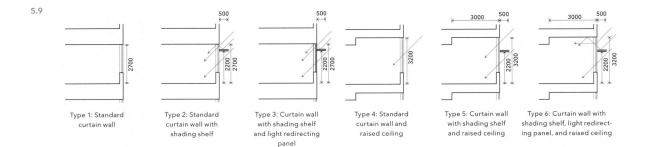

Type 1: Standard curtain wall

Type 2: Standard curtain wall with shading shelf

Type 3: Curtain wall with shading shelf and light redirecting panel

Type 4: Standard curtain wall and raised ceiling

Type 5: Curtain wall with shading shelf and raised ceiling

Type 6: Curtain wall with shading shelf, light redirecting panel, and raised ceiling

T 5.1

	TYPE 1	TYPE 2	TYPE 3	TYPE 4	TYPE 5	TYPE 6
LONDON						
North	7m	7m	6m	7.5m	8m	6.5m
East	7m	7.5m	7.5m	8.5m	8.5m	8.5m
South	12.5m	12.5m	10.5m	12m	14.5m	15.5m
West	8m	8.5m	8.5m	9.5m	9.5m	9m
DUBAI						
North	11m	11m	10m	13m	13m	11.5m
East	19m	19m	20m	20m	20m	20m
South	11.5m	11.5m	11m	13m	13.5m	13.5m
West	19m	19.5m	20m	20m	20m	20m
SINGAPORE						
North	4m	4.5m	4.5m	5.5m	5.5m	4.5m
East	8m	7m	6.5m	9m	9m	6.5m
South	5.5m	5m	5m	7m	6m	5m
West	10m	9m	10m	11.5m	11m	9m
SYDNEY						
North	11m	10.5m	11m	13m	9m	12.5m
East	15.5m	14.5m	14m	18m	15.5m	17.5m
South	10m	10m	8.5m	11m	9.5m	9.5m
West	12.5m	12m	12m	14m	12m	14m

5.10

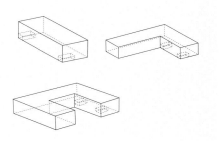

T 5.1 – Maximum depth of daylight penetration using a minimum *useful daylight illuminance* range between 250 lux and 2,000 lux

5.9 – Different types of window configurations and ceiling heights considered in Arney's study

5.10 – Three building formal typologies: Rectilinear, L-shape and U-shape

5.11 – Illustration of various combinations of building simulation conditions that were performed for variable site conditions in an urban context

5.11

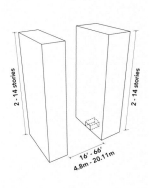

Effect of Opposite Building

The mere existence of a building facing a room with a side-wall window causes daylight levels to decrease by nearly 50% across the room. Figures 5.12a-c show the effect of three different heights of a building opposite the office room with a side-wall window and having a very low external skin light reflectance (1%). It is clear that the existence of such a building causes daylight levels to drop substantially throughout the room equipped with a side-wall window, whether it is a low-rise (a), mid-rise (b), or a high-rise building (c). In all three building heights, daylight factors dropped by as much as 50% in the front of the room and up to 70% in mid-zone when there is a building facing the test office compared to an unobstructed window in the test room.

Effect of Exterior Surface Reflectance of Opposite Building

The surface reflectance of an opposing building can make a measurable difference in the amount of light that enters a side-wall window across the street. Figure 5.13a-c illustrates the impact of opposite building reflectance on the performance of a side-wall window of a ground office, when the two buildings are separated by a one-lane street in the case of (a) low-rise, (b) mid-rise, and (c) high-rise buildings, respectively. The figures demonstrate that in all the three cases, as the exterior surface reflectance of the opposite building increases from 1% to 70%, the increase in the daylight levels inside the ground-floor office in the opposite building is substantial. These variations depend largely on density, however. Although a building opposite the room with a side-wall window obstructs a portion of the sky and, consequently, reduces daylights levels, the light loss could be minimized substantially if this building has a facade that has a high light reflectance.

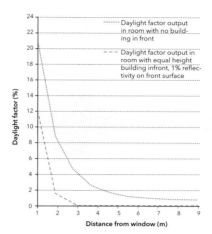

5.12a

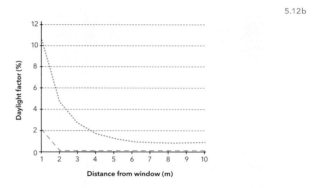

5.12b

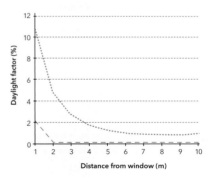

5.12c

T 5.2 – Matrix showing various combinations of building simulation conditions that were performed for variable site conditions in an urban context

5.12a-c – The effect of obstruction on daylight distribution inside a ground-floor office in the case of: (a) low-rise building; (b) mid-rise building; (c) high-rise building separated with a 4.88m wide (one-way) street in front

T 5.2

Building Type	Floor on Which Office is Located		Street Width			Height of Opposite Facing Building		Surface Reflectivity of Opposite Facing Building Façade	
	Ground Floor	Top Floor	One-Way, 4.88m wide	Two-Way, 7.6m wide	Four-Way, 20.12m wide	Equal Height of Original	Double Height of Original	1%	70%
Low-Rise, 2 stories (7.6m high)	•	•	•	•	•	•	•	•	•
Mid-Rise, 4 stories (15m high)	•	•	•	•	•	•	•	•	•
High-Rise, 14 stories (53m high)	•	•	•	•	•	•	•	•	•

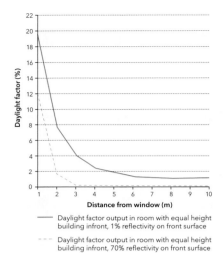

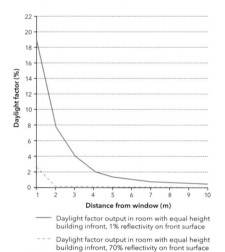

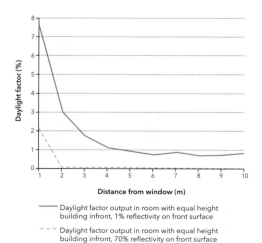

5.13a-c – The effect of opposite building surface reflectance on the daylight distribution inside a ground-floor office in the case of: (a) low-rise building; (b) mid-rise building; (c) high-rise building, respectively, with a 4.88m. wide one-lane street between them.

Effect of Distance between Buildings

The effect of urban density is governed not only by the height of surrounding buildings but also by the distance that separates buildings. In these simulations, three variables were investigated to examine the effect of distance between two opposite buildings, namely, the width of the street between two buildings, the height of the building where the test room is located, and the height of the building opposite the test room. Given a test room's location on the ground floor in a mid- or high-rise building, the street width dictated significant differences in the daylighting performance when the surface reflectance of the opposite building was nearly non-existent, or 1%. The daylight levels were nearly four times higher in the front of the room with a four-lane street compared to a one-lane street separating the two buildings. In the case of the existence of a mid- or high-rise building opposite the room with a side-wall window, a significant increase in light reflectance of the opposite building can alleviate, however, some of the light losses caused by the obstructing building 5.14a-b, 5.15a-b.

Effect of Building Form

Three formal building configurations were tested in these daylighting parametric simulations as shown in 5.12. Results generally indicate that building form has a considerable impact on the amount of daylight that reaches a side-wall window. The extent of the impact depends also on the location of a room within the building. The results of this study indicate that the same room equipped with a side-wall window in a rectilinear building receives more daylight than an identical room in a similar L-shaped or U-shaped building 5.16, 5.17. There could be a difference in the daylight factor of up to 50% between a corner office on the ground floor of a rectilinear building compared to the same corner office in an L-shaped or a U-shaped building of the same height.

The lessons learned from these studies are that the surrounding context, as defined by the building heights, street width, building exterior surface reflectance, and building shape play a very significant role in daylighting design and cannot be ignored by designers. Simple design tools and rules of thumb should not be the only methods depended upon for accurate design guidance.

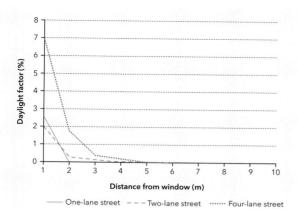

One-lane street   — — — Two-lane street   ·········· Four-lane street

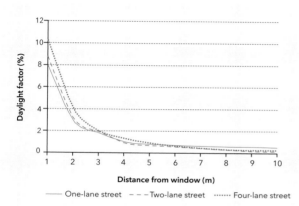

One-lane street   — — — Two-lane street   ·········· Four-lane street

5.14a-b – Street width effect on the daylighting performance of a side-wall window at a bottom-floor office in a mid-rise building with **(a)** 1% and **(b)** 70% external surface reflectance, respectively

5.15a-b – Street width effect on the daylighting performance of a side-wall window at a bottom-floor office in a high-rise building with: **(a)** 1% and **(b)** 70% external surface reflectance, respectively

5.16 – Comparison of daylighting performances between a linear, L-shape, and U-shape building of a ground-floor corner office with a side-wall window

5.17 – Effect of the horizontal location of a ground office with a side-wall window in a L-shape versus U-shape building on daylighting performance

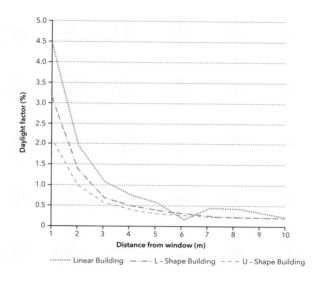

·········· Linear Building   — · — L – Shape Building   — — — U – Shape Building

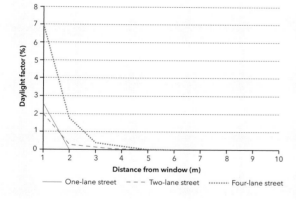

One-lane street   — — — Two-lane street   ·········· Four-lane street

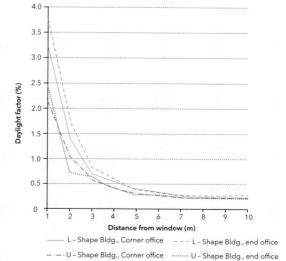

——— L – Shape Bldg., Corner office   — — — L – Shape Bldg., end office
— · — U – Shape Bldg., Corner office   ·········· U – Shape Bldg., end office

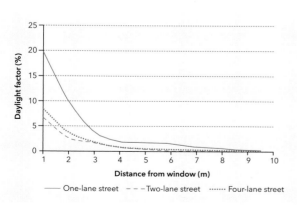

One-lane street   — — — Two-lane street   ·········· Four-lane street

CHAPTER 6

STRATEGIES AND SYSTEMS PERFORMANCE

There is a considerable amount of solar energy incident on the exterior surfaces of all buildings. On a clear day, there could be up to a 100,000 lumens incident on every square meter of the exterior walls or roof of a building. If these 100,000 lumens were captured and redistributed inside a building without any losses, one would need only 1m^2 of solar collection area to light 200m^2 of interior space at 500 lux or 400m^2 of interior space at 250 lux. No daylighting system is 100% efficient, however, and the majority of such systems, in fact, have an extremely low efficiency. The efficiency of the daylighting system is inversely proportional to the necessary light collection area and normally varies similar to cost. As efficiency decreases, the collection area must increase. With the example given above, if the efficiency were to drop to 10%, one would need 10 times the collection area to illuminate the same indoor floor area. The efficiency of any daylighting system is undoubtedly the biggest challenge. Unfortunately, the majority of daylighting systems suffer from low efficiency rates. High-efficiency systems tend to require fairly sophisticated technologies and as a result tend to be costly.

Experience seems to indicate that the best daylighting strategies cannot overcome a poorly designed building. The best solutions begin with a well-studied building shape, a sound organization of the spaces within the building, and a judicious placement of the building on its site and within its surroundings. As discussed in the previous chapter, building form can have a significant impact on its daylighting performance, and just like the floor plan, building form and placement can be the beginning of the problem or of a break-through solution.

Daylighting systems are broadly grouped into two categories based on the manner in which light is captured and distributed within a building. Sidelighting systems refer to systems that capture daylight and channel it inside through the openings in the wall of the building. Toplighting systems capture light and channel it inside from the top of a building.

Sidelighting Systems

The goal of all sidelighting systems is nearly always the same – capture sunlight or diffuse daylight incident on a building facade and redirect it toward the back portion of a room or the core of a large building where it is needed most. Therefore, a successful sidelighting strategy would provide a more balanced distribution of daylight throughout a room while minimizing glare and visual discomfort. Many of the sidelighting strategies tend to be relatively simple and, with a few exceptions, require mostly passive means.

Lightshelf

The lightshelf strategy is one of the most used side-lighting strategies today. A lightshelf is an apparatus placed between a window sill and a window head 6.1, 6.2. Although a lightshelf may be of many shapes, flat or curved, horizontal or inclined, most lightshelves tend to be flat, horizontal devices. While an inclined lightshelf can reflect light deeper into the room, it may present some water drainage problems. Interior curved lightshelves can reflect daylight over a wider area of the ceiling than flat shelves 6.3, 6.4. Lightshelves are considered more than just overhangs. An overhang would have only one role to play, which would be to shade a window. A lightshelf always divides a side window into two portions: the top portion, known as clerestory window, and the lower part, known as the view window. A lightshelf is judiciously placed within the window aperture to capture as much incident sunlight as possible and redirect it toward a highly reflective ceiling within a room, and ultimately from there into the middle and rear sections of the room. A lightshelf also can potentially improve the luminous quality of a room by increasing light levels in the back, lowering light levels in the front, and by cutting glare from the sky. A lightshelf also may play the simultaneous role of shading.

6.1 – Horizontal lightshelf
6.2 – Angled lightshelf
6.3 – Curved lightshelf
(Photo courtesy: © Hunter Douglas Contract)

6.4 – Curved lightshelf used in an elementary school (Photo courtesy: © Hunter Douglas Contract)

6.1

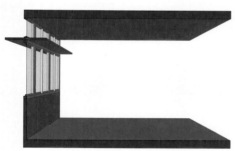

6.2

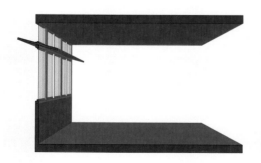

6.3

6.4

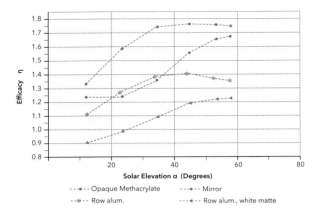

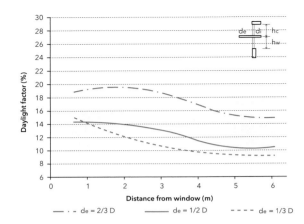

6.5 - Efficiency of a room with
a lightshelf with different surface
reflectances compared to same
room with simple window of the
same size according to solar
altitude (Courtesy: ©Elsevier)

6.6 - Curve-fitted daylight
distribution under diffuse clear
sky condition for three different
horizontal positions of the lightshelf with h_c = 1/3H; h_w=2/3H (H
being total height of the window
aperture)

6.7 - Curve-fitted daylight
distribution under diffuse clear
sky condition for three different
horizontal positions of the lightshelf with h_c = 1/2H; h_w=1/2H (H
being total height of the window
aperture)

6.8 - A variable area lightshelf
moving between two positions
to optimize daylight penetration
according to the sun's position
in the sky

6.9a-b - A variable area lightshelf moving between summer
position (a) and winter position
(b) to optimize daylight penetration

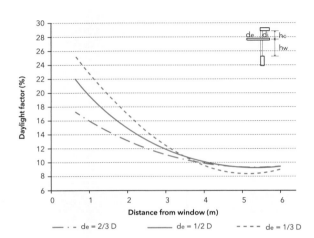

The amount of daylight that can be harvested and channeled into a room depends on such factors as the facade orientation, window and ceiling heights, the size and upper surface reflectance of the lightshelf, room surfaces, and sun angles. Because of the optical principle, it always is recommended that the upper surface of a lightshelf should be as reflective as possible even though mirrors are not typically recommended because they leave some bright spots in the ceiling which could cause discomfort. A comparison of different textures and reflective surfaces done in a three-year-long experimental investigation (Claros and Soler, 2001; Claros and Soler, 2002) concluded that a white matte surface seems to give the best year-long performance compared to mirror or aluminium surfaces 6.5. The same study suggested that a mirror lightshelf performed better during the two winter months when sun angles are low.

LS1 = row aluminium painted white matte
LS2 = opaque methacrylate
LS3 = mirror
LS4 = row aluminium.

The size, along with the vertical and horizontal positioning of the lightshelf affect the optics and the amount of light captured and redistributed. The depth of the lightshelf regulates how much light is harvested and redirected into the room. Having the external protrusion at least equal to or larger than the internal one (in the case of a combined lightshelf) provides better performance (Boubekri, 1992a; Boubekri, 1992b). Similarly, a lightshelf placed too high within the aperture leads to lower performance even under diffuse sky conditions 6.6, 6.7. A curved lightshelf tends to distribute light over a wider area than to a straight shelf. A study examining different lightshelf geometries combined with a curved ceiling found that an exterior curved shelf could improve daylight levels by as much as 10% compared to a horizontal lightshelf of the same size (Freewan, 2010).

Stationary lightshelves are likely to perform well only for a certain range of solar angles. As the sun angles change with the time of day and season, performance varies. To accommodate for changes in sun angles and to extend the optimal range of angles of incidence for which a lightshelf would perform optimally on an annual basis, a movable inclined lightshelf is suggested and is referred to as the variable area lightshelf (Littlefair, 1995). This arrangement consists of a reflective film that can slide along a railing on an inclined surface to adjust for sun angles. Its size changes by rolling over a cylinder 6.8, 6.9a-b. In doing so, reflection inside the room may be adjusted and maximized at all times on an annual basis. This system may be manually or automatically controlled.

There are no known measurements for the variable area lightshelf system. However, inclined lightshelves reflect light deeper into a room than those that are fixed and horizontal. Tests conducted at high latitudes in Norway found that a few degrees of inclination in the upward direction of an exterior lightshelf could lead to an increase of 55% daylight levels in the back of the room compared to a horizontal lightshelf of the same size (Arnesen, 2003).

Prismatic Panels

The use of prismatic glass is hardly a novelty in architectural lighting. It has been employed as a diffuser in the design of electric lighting fixtures to diffuse light and reduce glare. Its application in daylighting, however, has been not as extensive, mostly because a prism is not as transparent as glass, impeding a viewer to see through the window. With advances in prismatic film technology, today we observe an increase in its use in daylighting solutions.

Prisms come in a variety of sizes and shapes and can perform a wide range of functions. Prismatic panels may be rigid or flexible films. They may cover an entire facade 6.10, 6.11, applied as a film to a curtain wall system 6.12 or applied to a portion of a window aperture 6.13. They may be used as a light redirecting system in a side-daylighting application 6.14, 6.15 or they may be automated to play the dual role of shading and light redirecting according to the needs and seasons 6.16, 6.17. In its daylighting role, the system can be engineered to refract sunlight within a range of incident angles and channel light toward the rear section of a room. The prism angle, also known as prism vertex, and the angle of incidence of the incoming rays of light govern the angular deviation of the rays of light. As a result and depending on the position of the prism vertex, a prism also can provide shading by bending light in a downward direction 6.18.

Scale model testing 6.19 of the daylighting impact of clear acrylic prismatic panels attached to a window (Boubekri, 1999) reveals that such panels placed in the upper third portion of the window can lead to an enhanced daylight distribution across the room. This study also revealed that prism vertex influences the daylight distribution significantly 6.20. In this study, prism A and prism B refer to prisms shown in 6.15 and 6.18, respectively.

In its role as shading device, the prism angle orientation can be reversed and light can be deflected downward through natural refraction. This reversing mechanism of prismatic layers allows the system to play the dual roles of daylighting and shading by simply rotating the prism panels attached to the facade.

6.8

6.9a

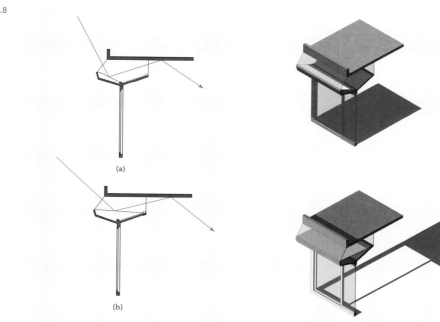

(a)

(b)

6.9b

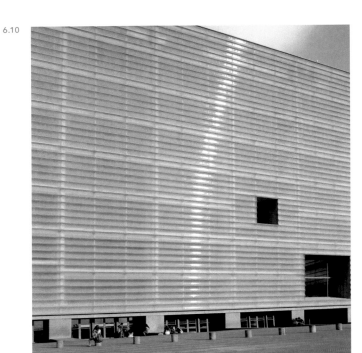

6.10 – Prismatic glass of the facade of Moneo's Kursaal Congress Palace in San Sebastian, Spain (Photo courtesy: Piedro)

6.11 – Exterior detail of the prismatic glass facade of the Kursaal Congress Palace, San Sebastian, Spain (Photo courtesy: Piedro)

6.12 – Prismatic curtain wall of the office tower of Comcast Center in Philadelphia, USA (Photo courtesy: Orlando O'Neil)

6.13 – A prismatic panel placed high in the window aperture reflects light off the ceiling and towards the back of the room

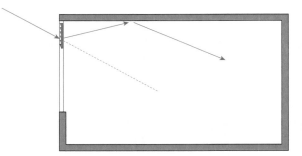

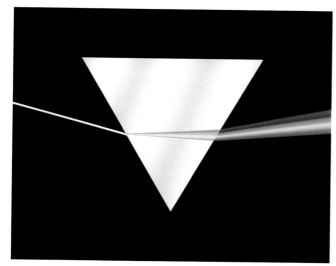

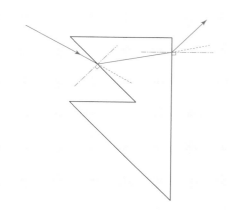

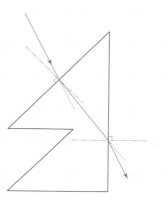

6.14 – Prism deflecting incoming light in an upward direction

6.15 – Light deviation in an upward direction increasing daylighting penetration in the back of the room

6.16 – Rotating prismatic panels at Sparkasse Fürstenfeldbruck, Germany, used for daylighting or as shading devices where sunlight may be deflected

in a downward direction (Photo: M. Boubekri)

6.17 – Prismatic panels can be rotated to defect light upward for daylighting or downward for shading (Photo: M. Boubekri)

6.18 – Shading prism deflecting light downward

6.19 – Longitudinal section across test scale model

Laser Cut Panels

Laser cut panels (LCPs) consist of an array of parallel equidistant cuts made by a laser cutting machine through a sheet of acrylic plastic 6.21. The laser cutting transforms the cut surface of the acrylic sheet to become highly polished and reflective. Compared to a typical louver system, the high density of the horizontal laser cuts allows a very high percentage of incoming light to be deflected upward. In addition to the density of the cuts, the transparency of the glass is maintained, resulting in a high light transmissivity of the LCP, unlike a typical louver system (Edmonds and Greenuo, 2002).

The basic optical principle of LCP is similar to many sidelighting systems. An incident ray of light is refracted into the material. A fraction of the incoming light reflects off the surface of a laser cut and is redirected upward 6.21-6.24.

6.20 – Comparison of the performance of 45° and 60° prismatic panels reflecting light in an upward direction (prism A) and a downward direction (prism B) under a clear sky condition

Laser cut panels can be used within side windows to redirect the incoming light away from the window and toward the ceiling and from there toward the rear section of the room.

The daylighting performance of an LCP depends on the angular relationship between the incident light and the inclination of the reflectors within the LCP (Edmonds, 1993). The angle of the cut plays an important role. A 19.2° angle of the cut availed better results than flat angle or a 7° angle according to a study conducted in Rio de Janeiro, Brazil 6.25. The improvements of the 19.2° degree LCP panel placed on the north side of a window were up to 190% better than a room with standard glass of equivalent transmittance.

A comparable experimental study conducted at a high latitude in Norway, using a 5m wide, 6m deep, and 3m high scale model prototype with laser cut panels at 10° angle in the upward direction, increased the daylight level by an average of 50% in the back section of the room opposite the window, compared to a similar prototype with a standard glass window.

6.20

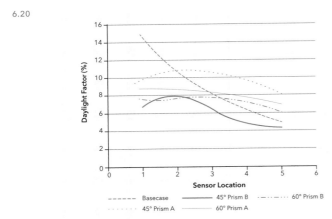

6.21

6.22

6.23

6.21 – The optical principle of a laser cut panel system (Courtesy: Ian Edmonds)

6.22 – A laser cut panel deflects light for deeper penetration but allows transparency and views (Photo courtesy: Ian Edmonds)

6.23 – A laser cut panel used in a side window in an elementary school in Brisbane, Australia (Photo courtesy: Ian Edmonds)

6.24 – Deflection of incoming daylight from the laser cut panels onto the ceiling used in a side window in an elementary school in Brisbane, Australia (Photo courtesy: Ian Edmonds)

6.25 – Daylighting performance of LCP cut at 0°, 7°, and 19.2° degree angles on June 21st at 12PM in Rio de Janeiro, Brazil, under CIE clear sky (Courtesy: © M. Laar)

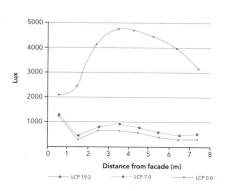

Anidolic Systems

Anidolic systems incorporate the non-imaging optical principles used in solar parabolic concentrators to capture daylight from the sky and the sun, concentrate the light into a focal point 6.26, then redistribute it into the interior of a building 6.27. Unlike many sidelighting systems that work best under sunny conditions, anidolic systems are able to perform well under overcast sky conditions because of their concentration factor due to the parabolic shape of the daylight harvesting system (Scartezzini and Courret, 2002; Courret et al., 1998; Courret, 1999). The concentration capability of this system can reach the theoretical limits of most concentrating optical systems, a maximum of 46,000 times for sunlight (Welford and Winston, 1989). This system can be designed to minimize reflections inside the concentrator 6.27, thereby minimizing light losses. Anidolic systems may accommodate a large spectrum of solar angles, making them appropriate for most geographical locations, for seasonal differences, and for a variety of building facade orientations.

Anidolic systems can be designed to be incorporated in new or refurbishment projects. The system can be placed on the top portion of the window 6.28 and may even be used in cases of refurbishment 6.29. In this case, the anidolic collector can collect and concentrate light and redirect it toward the section of the room opposite the window. It can be designed as an integral component of a room and be incorporated into the ceiling 6.28 to capture diffuse light or sunlight and by way of inter-reflection within the ceiling surfaces, it is channeled through the ceiling cavity and redistributed from an aperture in the ceiling placed in the middle portion or the rear section of the room opposite the window.

Window integrated anidolic collectors as well as ceiling integrated anidolic systems lead to significant improvements in daylight levels compared to a room with a standard window according to test measurements conducted at LESO-PB (Scartezzini and Courret, 2002; Courret et al., 1998). Enhancements of up to 70% in daylight levels in the middle and rear portion of the test room were achieved with these systems 6.30.

6.28

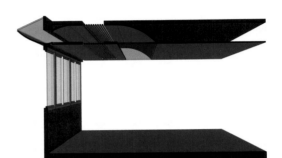

6.26

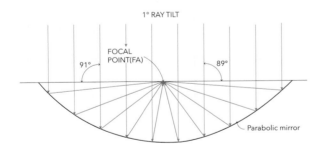

6.27

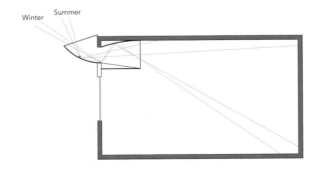

6.29

Louver Systems

A variety of louver systems used with side windows applications have been developed. The patented daylighting system "Daytec" developed by Bartenbach GmbH and manufactured by Durlum GmbH, Germany, is an optimized lamella system designed, according to the developer, to fulfill the following criteria:

- guide daylight into the depth of the building away from the window aperture 6.31, 6.32
- provide shading in summer and allow solar gains in winter
- reduce glare and enhance visual comfort for room occupants
- allow view to the outside.

6.26 – The profile of a concentrating parabolic mirror

6.27 – The profile of an anidolic system showing a parabolic-shaped concentrator (Courtesy: © Elsevier Limited).

6.28 – Anidolic collector placed on top of a standard side window and integrated with the ceiling

6.29 – Refurbished facade of the Laboratoire d'Energie Solaire et Physique du Bâtiment (LESO-PB) at Ecole Polytechnique Fédérale in Lausanne, Switzerland, using an anidolic sidelighting system (Photo courtesy: LESO-PB)

6.30 – Comparison of daylight factors achieved by the integrated anidolic ceiling, a slanted ceiling, and a conventional double glazing facade (Courtesy: © Elsevier Limited)

6.31 – Sketch of Daytec lamella system in casement window (a), blind detail (b), and view to the outside (c, d)

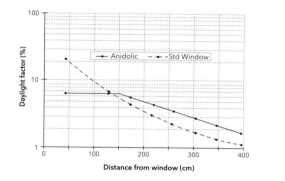

6.30

6.31a

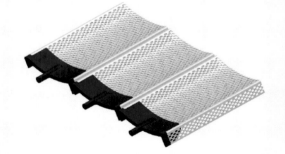

6.31b

6.31c

6.31d

In its "deflecting position" the concave shape together with a highly reflecting material allows redirection of daylight from the sky and the sun onto the ceiling and thus deep into the room 6.32. The side-mounting, as shown in 6.31-center, enables tilt angles of the blinds from 0° to 90° and, thus, a highly variable solar heat gain coefficient (SHGC). In this way the solar gains can be used in winter months and can be efficiently blocked in summer. To allow a view to the outside even for closed blinds, the lamellae in the direct field of view are elliptically perforated. Additionally, a sun-protecting film applied on the back side of the lamellae protects the user from glare. The installation inside a casement window protects the lamella system from dust and preserves the highly specular optical properties.

With the flexibility to freely arrange perforated and unperforated blinds, the facade can be split into an upper part for mainly daylight utilization and a lower part for the view to the outside and glare protection.

Figure 6.33 shows an example application where direct sunlight is used for illumination through the upper part of the system, whereas the lower part is in retro-position for sun shading.

The main advantage of the lamella system is the contact to the outside even in closed position. Due to 50% elliptical microperforation the view to the outside is comparable to a light-transmitting film if the user is at a distance where the eye cannot resolve the structure anymore 6.31. For the parts of the facade where no view is needed (e.g., above 1.80m) an unperforated type of the lamella is installed that increases the ability to redirect daylight into the room.

T 1 gives the optical properties of the perforated Daytec lamella system as installed in the mock-up. Together with the glazing the overall visual transmission in closed position is only 5%, which allows efficient glare protection.

6.32a

6.32

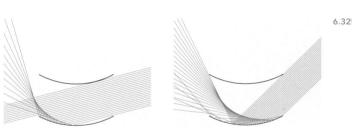

T 6.1

Visual transmission of film	17%
Perforation	50%
Visual transmission of caveat window (3+1 panes)	60%
Overall visual transmission	5%

6.33a–c

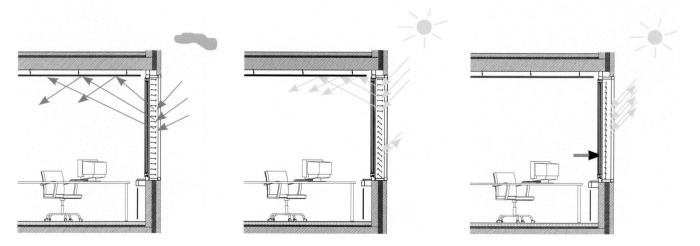

The images in 6.34 show the daylight system in a mock-up installation in glare protecting position, i.e., with blinds in closed position at 90° tilt angle. Although the sun hits the facade, the interior luminance at the inner side of the perforated lamellae is only 600cd/m², which is therefore a low glare level.

The ability to completely close the lamella system also allows a highly variable SHGC from as low as 5% (unperforated lamellae, closed position at 90° tilt angle) up to the SHGC of the glazing system in open position. Figure 6.35 shows angular dependent SHGCs for the perforated Daytec lamella system at various tilt angles of the blinds. The tilt angle of 45° (center) shows already low values for most of the upper hemisphere, the closed position (right) even yields low SHGCs for the perforated system 6.36.

Another louver system aiming at enhancing daylight distribution through side windows while controlling for

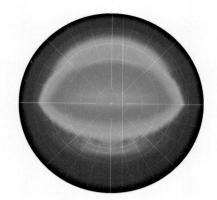

Tilt angle 0°

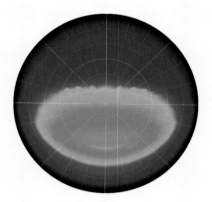

Tilt angle 45°

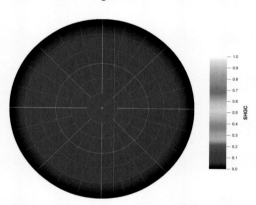

Tilt angle 90°

6.34a

6.34b

T 6.1 – Optical properties of the perforated Daytec lamella system in closed position (Courtesy: Bartenbach GmbH)

6.32 – Mock-up installation in test bed (a), ray paths in summer (b) and winter conditions (c)

6.33 – Working principle of Daytec lamellae: open, redirection position (a), retro position in the lower part and redirection position in the upper part (b), and closed position for sun shading with view to the outside (c)

6.34 – Evaluation of the mock-up installation with a luminance camera, tone-mapped HDR picture (a) and luminance false color representation (b)

6.35 – Angular dependent solar heat gain coefficients for various system positions of the perforated Daytec lamella system inside a casement window

unwanted solar heat gains is referred to as the Retrolux™ system shown in 6.36 and 6.37. As in all these side systems, the delicate balance between letting daylight in while blocking unwanted sunlight during the hot summer season must be maintained and provided to the user. The Retrolux™ system was designed to augment daylight distribution through a side window, reflect back to the outside unwanted solar rays, and improve the transparency of the lamella system. Depending on distance between the slats, the sun may reach only the exterior portion of the lamella which is itself shaped in V- or W-formation 6.36, 6.37. The resulting viewing transparency of this system in a horizontal position is about 74% 6.38 while allowing the majority of incident summer rays to be reflected back to the outside. The system may also be used in the upper part of a window as a lightshelf allowing the lower part of the window to be free for increased view to the outside or for sun-blocking system 6.39.

A third louver system, the LightLouver™ daylighting system, has been showcased extensively in chapter two of this book with the Manassas Park Elementary School (MPES). The LightLouver™ system is designed to optimize daylight penetration in winter and summer seasons as shown in 6.40. Using a patented, passive optical design, this louver system redirects all incoming sunlight deep into the space while eliminating glare and all direct sunlight penetration onto work surfaces. The lamellae or louvers are designed in the fish-bone shaped structure with highly reflective surfaces allowing sun rays to be inter-reflected between the inner and outer surfaces of the lamellae, at all angles of incidence above 5° as shown in 6.40. As a result, excellent daylighting and solar control for east, west, and south facing fenestration may be obtained.

This system is best used in the upper portion of the window aperture much like a lightshelf since it blocks nearly all view towards to the outside 6.41. LightLouver™ units are not recommended for north facing facades (+/- 30° of true north) because there is little direct sunlight on these facades except during early summer morning and late afternoon hours. LightLouver™ units might even reduce the annual amount of daylight entering the space from north facing windows even if they could balance the daylight distribution. LightLouver™ units are desirable in circumstances where the space function is extremely sensitive to direct sunlight such as art galleries or where functional or aesthetic requirements demand uniformity of light distribution.

6.36

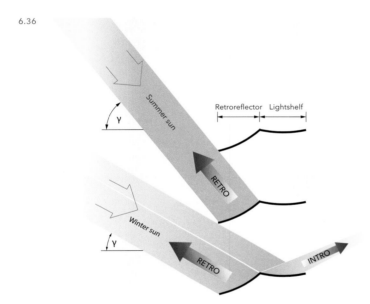

6.37

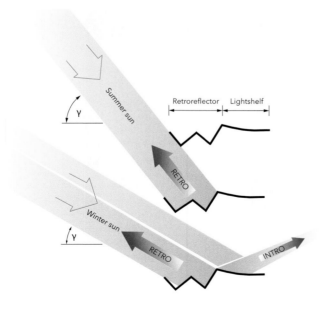

6.38

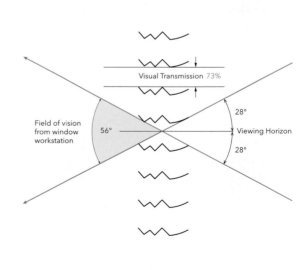

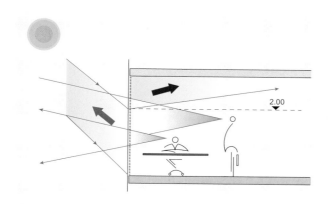

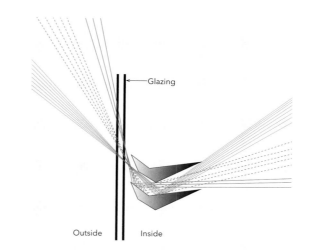

6.36 – V-shape Retrolux™ lamella system in summer and winter mode of operation (Courtesy: © Köster Lichtplanung)

6.37 – W-shape Retrolux™ lamella system in summer and winter mode of operation (Courtesy: © Köster Lichtplanung)

6.38 – Visual transmission through the W-lamella Retrolux™ system (Courtesy: © Köster Lichtplanung)

6.39 – Section detail showing the Retrolux™ system in a lightshelf mode placed in the upper part of the window aperture (Courtesy: © Köster Lichtplanung)

6.40 – Incoming sunlight being deflected by the LightLouver™ units in the upward direction toward the ceiling

6.41 – Close-up view of the LightLouver™ system (Photo courtesy: LightLouver™)

6.42 – LightLouver system used as a lightshelf in the upper section of a window (Photo: M. Boubekri)

Toplighting Systems

Top daylighting systems are designed to capture light generally on the roof of a building and channel the light into rooms below. These systems are especially desirable in core daylighting the core section of a large multistory building, where sidelighting may not be very efficient. Toplighting strategies vary from simple to highly sophisticated. They can involve automated solar trackers for collection, some sort of light transporters, and light distribution systems. Toplighting systems have the potential to bring more light inside a building because more daylight is available from the roof of a building than its sides during the course of an entire day. Toplighting systems are not affected by building orientation as much as sidelighting systems. They are, however, affected by the time factor, in that there is more daylight available at mid-day than at any other time of the day. They are also affected by the changes in the seasons. During the summer, sun angles are high and, consequently, more solar radiation is available on a horizontal surface than during the winter days when the sun angles are comparatively lower.

As discussed in chapter 5, the distance from the windows is a major problem in a typical sidelighting application, causing the core section of a building to be quite dark and to rely on electric lighting. There are other reasons for relying on electric lighting in core sections of a building that go beyond just the distance from windows (Garcia-Hansen and Edmonds, 2003). The large disparities in illuminance levels between peripheral and sections of a building far away from windows create an unpleasant and cave-like atmosphere. Windows often can lead to reflected glare, direct glare, or discomfort glare problems. When windows are small, the glare issue is related to discomfort glare caused by the large contrast between the bright window and its surrounding darker walls. When windows are large, there could be other types of glare such as veiling reflections or reflected glare due to excessive sunlight penetration. Toplighting can be an effective strategy to compensate for many such problems.

6.43 – Two-story deep skylights at Terminal 3, Zurich International Airport, Switzerland (Photo: M. Boubekri)

6.44 – Efficiency factors for various proportions (well index) of the skylight wells based on well inter-reflectance values (© *Illuminating Engineering Society of North America*.)

6.45 – Series of skylights at Barajas International Airport, Madrid, Spain (Photo: M. Boubekri)

Skylights

Skylights are among the simplest and most used of daylighting strategies. They are simple openings in the roof that admit daylight inside a building 6.43. Skylights frequently are employed in residential buildings in cold climates where overcast skies prevail. Toplighting in general is more suitable than sidelighting under overcast skies because the sky luminance of the zenithal portion of the sky is nearly three times higher than sky luminance at the horizon. Multiple skylights generally provide a more uniform daylight distribution across the space than a single skylight 6.45.

The efficiency of a skylight represents the ratio or percentage between the luminous energy leaving the bottom of the skylight well and the total luminous energy incident on it before it enters the skylight system. Much of the skylight efficiency is dictated by the skylight well size, wall reflectances, and the light transmittance of the glazed cover.

For straight rectilinear skylights, efficiencies are published in the Handbook of the Illuminating Engineering Society of North America 6.44. The Well Index (WI) characterizes the proportional relationships between width, length, and depth of the skylight well and it is calculated as follows:

$$WI = \frac{Well\ Height\ x\ (Well\ Length + Well\ Width)}{2\ x\ Well\ Length\ x\ Well\ Width}$$

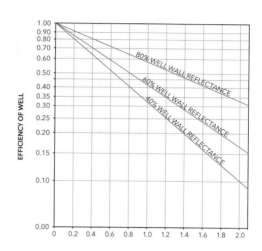

6.44

6.45

77

In splayed skylights with a pyramidal light well 6.46, the splay angle is an additional factor that affects the overall efficiency of the skylight system (Mistrick, 2006). A parametric study involving computer and scale model simulations provided efficiency values for various depths and angles of the splayed skylight wells that have a square base and opening. Skylight well efficiencies were generated for various splay angles ranging from 30° to 90°, for different reflectances of the inner surfaces of the well walls, and also for varying depths T6.1, 6.2, 6.3, 6.4 (Boubekri and Anninos, 1995).

The lessons learned were that, as a general rule, as the splay angle increases, the effective reflectance of the top opening has a greater effect on the well efficiency, particularly when the play angle is above 60°. This suggests that higher effective reflectances should be used for large splay angles. Based on the results of this study, the two most noticeable trends are that the well efficiency increases as the wall reflectance increases for any given height-to-width ratio. The well efficiency decreases as the well height-to-width ratio increases. The latter is the most potent factor that affects skylight efficiency. The effect of well wall reflectance is, however, not as significant for small splay angles as it is for large angles. For a 45° skylight with equal height and width (H/W = 1), an increase in the wall reflectance from 10% to 80% results in an increase in well efficiency of 26%. For a 90° splay angle and the same height-to-width ratio, the efficiency of the skylight more than doubles.

For round skylights, efficiency ratios were established by Tsangrassoulis and Santamouris (2000) using the same flux transfer method as in Boubekri's study for splayed skylights (Boubekri, 1995). The variables examined compared the ratio of the depth of the skylight well to the radius of the round base (H/r) and the reflectance of its surfaces. For diffuse skylights, these efficiency ratios are presented in T6.5 for various well wall reflectances and a 40% reflectance of the bottom glazing ($\rho_3 = 0.4$). Under sunny conditions the efficiency ratios are shown in T6.6, T6.7, 6.47 for well walls reflectances (ρ_2) of 20% and 80%, respectively, and various sun elevation angles.

6.46

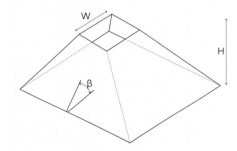

6.46 – Splayed skylight well with a square opening

T6.1 – Well efficiency for a 30° angled well with a square base and opening

T6.2 – Well efficiency for a 45° angled well with a square base and opening

T6.3 – Well efficiency for a 60° angled well with a square base and opening

T6.4 – Well efficiency for a 90° angled well with a square base and opening

T6.1

H/W	Well Wall Reflectance (%)							
	10	20	30	40	50	60	70	80
0.25	0.931	0.939	0.946	0.954	0.961	0.969	0.977	0.985
0.50	0.899	0.909	0.920	0.931	0.942	0.953	0.965	0.977
0.75	0.879	0.891	0.904	0.917	0.930	0.943	0.958	0.972
1.00	0.867	0.880	0.893	0.907	0.922	0.937	0.952	0.969
1.25	0.857	0.871	0.886	0.901	0.916	0.933	0.950	0.967
1.50	0.850	0.865	0.880	0.596	0.912	0.929	0.947	0.966
1.75	0.845	0.860	0.876	0.592	0.909	0.927	0.945	0.965
2.00	0.841	0.856	0.872	0.589	0.906	0.924	0.944	0.964

T6.3

H/W	Well Wall Reflectance (%)							
	10	20	30	40	50	60	70	80
0.25	0.817	0.833	0.849	0.866	0.884	0.902	0.922	0.943
0.50	0.706	0.728	0.752	0.777	0.804	0.834	0.866	0.900
0.75	0.633	0.658	0.686	0.716	0.749	0.785	0.825	0.870
1.00	0.582	0.609	0.638	0.671	0.708	0.749	0.795	0.848
1.25	0.544	0.571	0.602	0.637	0.676	0.721	0.772	0.831
1.50	0.515	0.543	0.574	0.610	0.650	0.698	0.753	0.817
1.75	0.492	0.520	0.552	0.588	0.631	0.680	0.738	0.807
2.00	0.474	0.502	0.534	0.-170	0.614	0.664	0.725	0.797

T6.2

H/W	Well Wall Reflectance (%)							
	10	20	30	40	50	60	70	80
0.25	0.879	0.891	0.903	0.915	0.928	0.941	0.955	0.969
0.50	0.811	0.828	0.846	0.865	0.884	0.905	0.926	0.949
0.75	0.768	0.788	0.809	0.831	0.855	0.880	0.907	0.936
1.00	0.738	0.760	0.783	0.808	0.834	0.863	0.894	0.927
1.25	0.716	0.739	0.764	0.790	0.819	0.850	0.884	0.920
1.50	0.699	0.723	0.749	0.777	0.807	0.840	0.876	0.916
1.75	0.686	0.711	0.737	0.766	0.797	0.832	0.870	0.912
2.00	0.676	0.700	0.727	0.727	0.789	0.825	0.865	0.909

T6.4

H/W	Well Wall Reflectance (%)							
	10	20	30	40	50	60	70	80
0.25	0.652	0.672	0.693	0.716	0.741	0.768	0.797	0.830
0.50	0.437	0.460	0.486	0.515	0.548	0.586	0.630	0.682
0.75	0.301	0.321-	0.347	0.356	0.410	0.451	0.501	0.563
1.00	0.215	0.233	0.253	0.279	0.310	0.350	0.400	0.467
1.25	0.158	0.172	0.190	0.211	0.239	0.274	0.322	0.389
1.50	0.120	0.131	0.145	0.163	0.186	0.217	0.261	0.325
1.75	0.093	0.102	0.113	0.'128	0.147	0.174	0.213	0.273
2.00	0.074	0.081	0.090	0.102	0.118	0.140	0.175	0.230

Atrium

The atrium is a form of a large light well that, when incorporated within a building, allows the core area that otherwise receives little or no daylight to be adequately daylit. This daylighting strategy can be especially useful in internally load-dominated medium or large size office or commercial buildings where the core is far away from the exterior walls.

In the past few decades, the atrium has become a ubiquitous design feature in many office buildings, malls, and shopping centers. An atrium supplies daylight to the spaces adjacent to the atrium in addition to illuminating the core of the building with daylight. When properly designed, an atrium can serve as a pleasurable visual amenity, and a thermal buffer zone between the exterior environment and interior of a building allowing ventilation to take place using the air movement from stack effect.

One of the most important daylighting characteristics of an atrium is its generic shape and its fenestration system. Beyond the cubical or rectilinear type, there are other forms. As contemporary buildings become more and more like sculptural pieces, their atria can take almost any shape. Within the generic rectilinear form, taxonomy was developed in the 1980s to identify the type of atrium according to the location of the atrium in relation to the rest of the building and to the number of its open sides (Saxon, 1983). The four-sided atrium would be enclosed from four sides and have a glass top cover 6.48. The three-sided atrium would have a glass cover top and a glazed side 6.50. The two-sided or linear atrium would have a glass cover and two open ends where light comes into the building 6.49. These are the generic taxonomies but there could be a wide range of variations in terms of location of glass, etc.

Daylight distribution within an atrium depends more on its dimensional proportions rather than its actual size. The proportional relationships between its various dimensions in the case of a rectilinear atrium are described by numerous geometric indices such as the Plane Aspect Ratio (PAR), the Section Aspect Ratio (SAR), the ratio between atrium height and its width, the room index (RI), or the well index (WI) as shown in 6.51, 6.52.

T 6.5 – Round skylight efficiency (%) for various values of aspect ratio (H/r) and wall reflectance ($\rho_3 = 0.4$)

T 6.6 – Round skylight efficiency (%) for various values of aspect ratio (H/r) and sun elevation (wall reflectance $\rho_2 = 0.4$)

T 6.7 – Round skylight efficiency (%) for various values of aspect ratio (H/r) and sun elevation (wall reflectance $\rho_2 = 0.8$)

6.47 – Round skylight efficiencies as a function of the aspect ratio H/r for various values of solar elevations (wall reflectance $\rho_2 = 0.2$) (Courtesy: © Elsevier Limited)

T 6.5

H / r	$r_2 = 0.2$	$r_2 = 0.4$	$r_2 = 0.6$	$r_2 = 0.8$
0.2	31.4	37.4	43.7	51
0.5	20.9	22.3	23.7	25.2
1	12.6	13	13.3	13.7
2	5.5	5.6	5.7	5.75
4	1.7	1.8	1.8	1.9
8	0.48	0.48	0.48	0.49

T 6.6

H / r	10°	30°	50°	70°	90°
0.2	0.77	13.27	27.36	36.13	41.25
0.5	0.37	7.37	20.77	30.90	38.05
1	0.14	0.88	13.27	26.21	37.09
2	0.04	0.36	2.06	18.45	36.74
4	0.01	0.10	0.25	5.49	36.66
8	0.0033	0.02	0.065	0.15	36.64

T 6.7

H / r	10°	30°	50°	70°	90°
0.2	0.86	14.88	30.67	40.49	46.23
0.5	0.76	7.53	21.36	31.79	39.14
1	0.28	0.88	13.38	26.43	37.40
2	0.09	0.73	2.06	18.49	36.80
4	0.02	0.20	0.50	5.47	36.67
8	0.006	0.05	0.13	0.30	36.65

6.47

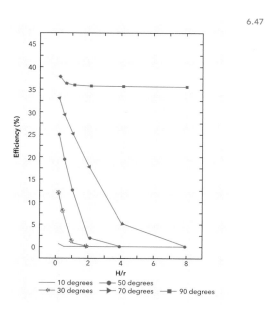

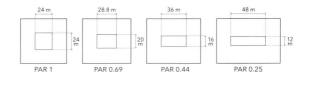

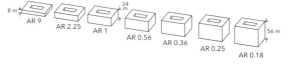

6.48 – Interior view of the four-sided atrium of the Hilton-Anatole Hotel in Dallas, Texas, USA (Photo: M. Boubekri)

6.49 – Linear atrium of Temple Buell Hall, University of Illinois at Urbana-Champaign, USA (Photo: M. Boubekri)

6.50 – Three-sided atrium of the UPC Building in Leeuwarden, the Netherlands (Photo courtesy: Paul de Ruiter Architects)

6.51 – Four-sided atria with different Plan Aspect Ratios (PAR) and Section Aspect Ratios (SAR)

6.52 – Examples of different well indexes and Aspect ratios

6.53 – The critical locations inside a four-sided atrium where DEFs were calculated

T 6.8 – DEF (%) in a four-sided atrium at the critical locations inside the atrium (as indicated in 6.52)

T 6.9 – DEF (%) in a four-sided atrium at the center of its shorter walls (point P_8 as indicated in 6.53)

For an atrium of given length (L), width (W), and height (H), these ratios are:

$$SAR = \frac{Well\ Height}{Well\ Width} = \frac{H}{W}$$

$$PAR = \frac{Well\ Width}{Well\ Length} = \frac{W}{L}$$

$$WI = \frac{Well\ Height\ x\ (Well\ Length + Well\ Width)}{2\ x\ Well\ Length\ x\ Well\ Width}$$

Daylight efficiency factors (DEF) have been developed for different locations along the walls and floor of three generic cubical types of atria, namely: four-sided, three-sided, and linear atrium using flux transfer theory which assumes diffuse conditions within the atrium (Boubekri and Anninos, 1996 a, b; Anninos and Boubekri, 1996) 6.53-6.55, T 6.8-6.9. DEF illustrates the effect of atrium dimensional proportions and reflectance of the surface reflectances of the atrium walls of the atrium.

For a cube shaped atrium (PAR = SAR = 1), the daylight efficiency factor (DEF) at the center of one of the unglazed walls is only 30.5% for a four-sided atrium

T 6.9. For a three-sided atrium, the DEF is 29.7% at the center of the unglazed wall T 6.10. For a linear atrium, the DEF at the center of one of the two unglazed walls is 23.3% T 6.11. The average light reflectance of the inner surfaces of the atrium in all the three types of atria discussed is assumed to be 50%. The loss of light is due to the atrium surface reflectances and its dimensions. Proportional relationships have also a significant impact on the light loss within the atrium, with the SAR having the largest impact. These DEFs do not account for the atrium glass transmittance or roof canopy transmittance, which are additional variables to be taken into account in determining the overall light loss.

Using scale models, the effective transmittance (ET) of 36 different canopy systems covering a four-sided atrium was measured in a sky simulator simulating the International Commission on Illumination (CIE) standard overcast sky conditions (Song, 2007). Among the canopy systems tested were various sawtooth systems, barrel vaults, pyramidal and flat horizontal skylights as shown in 6.56. The results of the scale model testing are indicated in T 6.12. It is important to mention that the values of ET in this study were measured not just underneath the roof canopy but at seven locations on the bottom floor of the atrium. The values of ET were extrapolated based on daylight measurements at the same seven locations on the floor of the same atrium without a canopy. The lowest average transmittance value registered was 5.39% for the sawtooth system (type 09) and the highest average value was 75.06% for pyramidal skylight (type 25) 6.56.

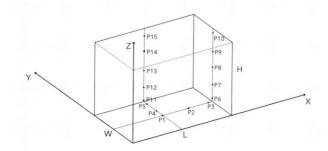

T 6.8

PAR	Wall reflec.	SAR						
		0.5	0.75	1.0	1.5	2.0	3.0	4.0
0.2	0.7	53.7	48.8	44.5	37.4	31.8	23.6	17.9
	0.5	49.1	42.8	37.7	29.8	24.1	16.6	12.0
	0.3	45.3	38.2	32.6	24.6	19.3	12.8	9.81
0.4	0.7	53.3	48.1	43.5	35.8	29.7	20.9	15.0
	0.5	48.6	42.0	36.5	28.1	22.1	14.2	9.48
	0.3	44.8	37.3	31.5	23.0	17.4	10.6	6.81
0.6	0.7	52.6	46.9	41.9	33.5	27.1	18.0	12.2
	0.5	47.8	40.7	34.8	25.8	19.5	11.6	7.23
	0.3	43.8	35.9	29.7	20.8	15.0	8.32	4.91
0.8	0.7	51.7	45.4	40.0	31.1	24.4	15.4	9.99
	0.5	46.6	39.0	32.7	23.3	17.0	9.44	5.56
	0.3	42.5	34.1	27.6	18.5	12.7	6.49	3.58
1.0	0.7	50.6	43.8	38.0	28.6	21.9	13.2	8.21
	0.5	45.2	37.1	30.5	20.9	14.7	7.71	4.33
	0.3	41.0	32.2	25.4	16.2	10.7	5.10	2.67

T 6.9

Location	P₁	P₂	P₃	P₄	P₅
DEF(%)	23.7	22.0	17.5	23.0	21.3
Location	P₆	P₇	P₈	P₉	P₁₀
DEF(%)	11.3	15.1	22.1	34.8	58.7
Location	P₁₁	P₁₂	P₁₃	P₁₄	P₁₅
DEF(%)	10.7	14.4	22.2	36.7	58.8

PAR	Wall reflectance	Glazing location	SAR						
			0.5	0.75	1.0	1.5	2.0	3.0	4.0
0.4 (S)	0.7	Top Gl. Side Gl.	53.9 3.71	48.1 6.11	42.7 8.53	33.5 13.0	26.4 16.8	16.7 22.4	10.9 25.9
	0.5	Top Gl. Side Gl.	50.4 3.33	43.6 5.29	37.5 7.17	27.7 10.5	20.7 13.1	11.9 16.6	7.23 18.6
0.6 (S)	0.7	Top Gl. Side Gl.	50.9 8.03	44.0 12.5	38.0 16.5	28.3 23.4	21.2 28.6	12.5 35.3	7.64 39.2
	0.5	Top Gl. Side Gl.	47.7 7.36	40.0 11.1	33.4 14.4	23.5 19.5	16.8 23.1	9.04 27.4	51.9 29.6
0.8 (S)	0.7	Top Gl. Side Gl.	47.9 12.3	40.2 18.4	33.7 23.7	24.0 31.9	17.4 37.7	9.57 44.7	5.57 48.4
	0.5	Top Gl. Side Gl.	44.8 11.4	36.4 16.6	29.7 20.8	20.0 30.0	13.8 31.0	7.05 35.5	3.89 37.6
1.0	0.7	Top Gl. Side Gl.	45.1 15.8	36.9 23.1	30.2 29.2	20.7 38.2	14.5 44.1	7.58 51.1	4.24 54.4
	0.5	Top Gl. Side Gl.	42.1 14.5	33.3 20.7	26.6 25.5	17.3 32.3	11.6 36.5	5.68 40.9	3.03 42.8
0.8 (L)	0.7	Top Gl. Side Gl.	46.8 16.6	37.9 24.3	31.5 30.6	22.1 40.2	15.9 46.6	8.74 54.2	6.00 58.1
	0.5	Top Gl. Side Gl.	43.1 15.5	34.7 22.1	28.2 27.3	19.1 34.8	13.3 39.5	6.89 44.6	3.86 47.1
0.6 (L)	0.7	Top Gl. Side Gl.	46.3 17.4	38.7 25.3	32.5 32.0	23.5 42.1	17.4 49.0	10.0 57.3	6.23 61.7
	0.5	Top Gl. Side Gl.	43.9 16.3	36.0 23.4	29.7 29.0	20.1 39.2	15.1 42.4	8.43 48.4	5.03 51.5
0.4 (L)	0.7	Top Gl. Side Gl.	46.6 18.0	39.3 26.2	33.4 33.1	24.7 43.6	18.9 50.8	11.7 59.8	7.71 64.7
	0.5	Top Gl. Side Gl.	44.5 17.0	36.9 244	30.9 30.4	22.5 39.2	16.9 45.0	10.3 51.8	5.77 40.9

T 6.10 – DEF (%) due to top-light and the side light at point P_{15} in a three-sided atrium (6.54) for different PAR and SAR configurations

T 6.11 – DEF (%) due to top-light and the side light at point P_8 (6.55) in a linear atrium for different PAR and SAR configurations

T 6.12 – Effective transmittance of 36 canopies for overcast skies

6.54 – The critical locations inside a three-sided atrium where DEFs were calculated

6.55 – The critical locations inside a two-sided linear atrium where DEFs were calculated

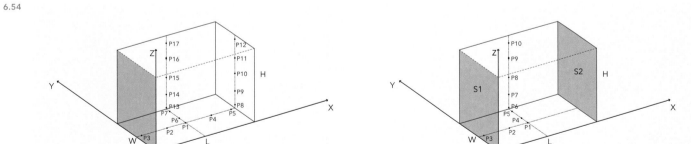

6.54

6.55

PAR	Wall reflec.	Glazing	SAR						
			0.5	0.75	1.0	1.5	2.0	3.0	4.0
0.2	0.7	Top Gl. Side Gl.	55.7 0.70	50.8 1.26	46.2 1.90	37.8 3.32	30.9 4.70	20.9 7.10	14.5 8.91
	0.5	Top Gl. Side Gl.	52.1 0.62	46.1 1.05	40.5 1.52	31.3 2.47	24.3 3.36	15.2 4.79	9.81 5.81
0.4	0.7	Top Gl. Side Gl.	52.5 3.62	46.1 5.88	40.2 8.09	30.4 12.1	23.2 15.2	13.8 19.5	8.56 22.1
	0.5	Top Gl. Side Gl.	49.6 3.27	42.4 5.16	36.2 6.95	26.2 9.98	19.2 12.3	10.7 15.3	6.27 16.9
0.6	0.7	Top Gl. Side Gl.	48.3 7.66	4.06 11.6	34.0 15.0	24.1 20.4	17.3 24.1	9.42 28.6	5.45 30.8
	0.5	Top Gl. Side Gl.	46.1 7.14	38.0 10.0	31.2 13.5	21.3 17.9	14.8 20.8	7.61 24.1	4.22 25.6
0.8	0.7	Top Gl. Side Gl.	44.1 11.4	35.6 16.4	28.9 20.5	19.4 26.3	13.4 29.9	6.83 33.9	3.79 35.7
	0.5	Top Gl. Side Gl.	42.5 10.8	33.7 15.4	26.9 18.9	17.5 23.8	11.7 29.8	5.70 29.8	3.06 31.1
1.0	0.7	Top Gl. Side Gl.	40.3 14.0	31.4 19.6	24.8 23.8	15.9 29.5	10.7 32.9	5.24 36.3	2.82 37.9
	0.5	Top Gl. Side Gl.	39.0 13.4	30.0 18.5	23.3 22.3	14.6 27.2	9.51 30.0	4.48 32.7	2.34 33.8

Canopy no.	Atrium well index							Ave. ET (%)
	0.6	0.9	1.2	1.5	1.8	2.1	2.4	
01	9.78	9.81	9.51	9.11	9.60	9.27	9.52	9.51
02	15.17	15.59	15.45	15.30	15.50	14.35	14.72	15.15
03	20.38	20.72	20.51	20.31	19.49	19.o7	20.35	20.12
04	24.15	23.85	24.67	25.05	25.32	23.71	25.22	24.57
05	8.37	8.33	8.18	8.35	8.32	7.66	8.12	8.19
06	13.93	14.16	13.79	13.85	13.37	12.57	13.53	13.60
07	20.12	20.30	19.89	20.15	20.55	18.98	20.02	20.00
08	23.97	24.43	24.67	24.35	23.54	23.26	24.57	24.11
09	5.84	5.89	5.52	5.17	4.84	5.17	5.30	5.39
10	12.31	12.37	11.96	12.23	11.17	10.78	11.15	11.71
11	17.27	17.32	16.82	16.81	15.65	15.69	14.83	16.34
12	21.90	22.15	21.55	21.55	20.91	19.88	19.26	21.03
13	46.15	45.31	46.45	46.71	48.79	45.10	46.86	46.48
14	42.25	41.75	41.63	41.41	40.40	42.16	41.61	41.60
15	35.40	35.37	35.32	34.35	33.25	34.31	34.42	34.63
16	28.71	28.96	29.13	27.72	27.12	27.54	27.87	28.15
17	62.68	66.12	67.94	68.91	68.07	64.35	65.48	66.22
18	54.69	57.76	59.14	60.13	59.39	57.04	56.71	57.84
19	30.23	31.94	33.10	33.46	33.36	31.73	32.03	32.26
20	15.53	16.23	16.40	16.76	16.57	15.95	15.58	16.15
21	64.15	66.39	66.69	66.27	66.86	63.81	65.69	65.70
22	55.39	57.10	56.56	56.41	56.76	54.55	55.41	56.02
23	30.72	31.45	31.15	31.20	31.58	31.46	31.39	31.28
24	14.84	15.68	15.28	15.57	16.00	16.49	15.91	15.68
25	70.75	75.05	76.16	76.08	76.74	77.81	72.84	75.06
26	60.23	63.54	66.20	64.98	65.15	66.76	62.66	64.22
27	32.80	34.85	35.59	35.40	35.42	35.92	33.55	34.79
28	15.84	16.13	16.53	16.43	16.71	16.76	16.02	16.35
29	53.70	57.46	61.38	65.41	67.78	67.47	64.29	62.50
30	35.03	40.23	44.77	49.89	52.77	54.63	52.71	47.15
31	23.02	26.28	30.73	36.05	38.62	41.09	40.37	33.74
32	16.25	19.63	23.63	27.91	30.94	34.31	34.20	26.70
33	57.12	60.29	63.46	67.62	69.56	70.14	67.42	65.09
34	43.51	47.86	51.74	56.73	58.25	60.43	59.20	53.96
35	27.91	32.06	36.17	40.09	42.96	45.63	44.91	38.53
36	17.98	21.12	25.00	28.61	32.08	34.94	36.15	27.98

TOP VIEWS AND SECTIONS OF CANOPY SYSTEMS
SAWTOOTH CANOPIES WITH VERTICAL APERTURES

2 - UNIT   4 - UNIT   8 - UNIT

South

500mm

500mm

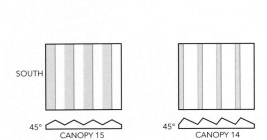

CANOPY 01   CANOPY 05   CANOPY 09

CANOPY 02   CANOPY 06   CANOPY 10

CANOPY 03   CANOPY 07   CANOPY 11

CANOPY 04   CANOPY 08   CANOPY 12

SAWTOOTH CANOPIES WITH SLOPED APERTURES

800mm

SOUTH

500mm

15° CANOPY 13

30° CANOPY 14

SOUTH

45° CANOPY 15

45° CANOPY 14

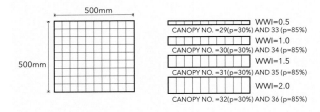

500mm

500mm

WWI=0.5
CANOPY NO. =29(p=30%) AND 33 (p=85%)

WWI=1.0
CANOPY NO. =30(p=30%) AND 34 (p=85%)

WWI=1.5
CANOPY NO. =31(p=30%) AND 35 (p=85%)

WWI=2.0
CANOPY NO. =32(p=30%) AND 36 (p=85%)

FLAT HORIZONTAL SKYLIGHTS

500mm

500mm

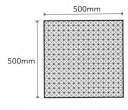

CANOPY NO.
NO GLAZING = 17
CLEAR TRANSPARENT = 18
TINTED TRANSPARENT = 19
WHITE TRANSLUCENT = 20

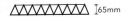 65mm

BARREL VAULT SKYLIGHTS

500mm

South
500mm

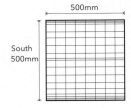

CANOPY NO.
NO GLAZING = 21
CLEAR TRANSPARENT = 22
TINTED TRANSPARENT = 23
WHITE TRANSLUCENT = 24

PYRAMID SKYLIGHTS

500mm

500mm

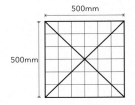

CANOPY NO.
NO GLAZING = 25
CLEAR TRANSPARENT = 26
TINTED TRANSPARENT = 27
WHITE TRANSLUCENT = 28

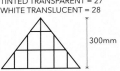

300mm

6.56 – Various roof canopy
configuration for which effective
transmittance was measured
for overcast sky conditions
(Courtesy: © Sage Publications)

Lightpipes

As a toplighting strategy, lightpipes are designed to channel daylight into the lower floors or the core area of a multistory building. There are three components to a lightpipe: a collector, a transport, and a distribution system. Lightpipes can be of different types and sizes. The light collection system may be a simple hole in the roof covered with a clear polycarbonate dome 6.57, a stationary or solar tracking mirror (heliostat) 6.58, an optical lens, or a light deflector such as a laser cut panel. Light transport systems may consist of hollow mirrored ducts or coated inside with anodized aluminium or coated plastics that can attain reflectance values as high as 99%. Other possible light transport mechanisms may be hollow prism light guides, collimating or focusing lenses, or fiber optics 6.59. There are as many types of lightpipes as there are possible combinations of all these systems and sub-systems. With such a diversity of types and sizes of lightpipes, it would be nearly impossible to examine or report on the efficiency of all these potential combinations in a way that can be comprehensive and succinctly summarized.

Hollow Mirror Lightpipes

Hollow mirrored lightpipes are the most widely available types on the market. They are found in residential and commercial buildings. With hollow mirror lightpipes, light is transported by internal reflections. In addition to the duct's aperture and length, the angle of entry of the ray of light and the reflectance of the inner surface of the duct play the most important roles in determining efficiency. A small angle of entry minimizes the number of reflections and increases efficiency.

With an aspect ratio (length/width) of 4, 99% internal reflectance, and a clear polycarbonate dome as a collector, the daylight penetration factor (DPF) from a lightpipe was found to exceed 0.2% for the majority of winter and summer days 6.60a-b inside a 9 m^2 windowless test room with a height of 2m (Paroncini et al., 2007). The DPF is a concept proposed in 2005 by Zhang and Muneer (2005) to assess the performance of lightpipes. It was defined as the ratio of the average indoor illuminance to the outdoor horizontal illuminance:

6.57

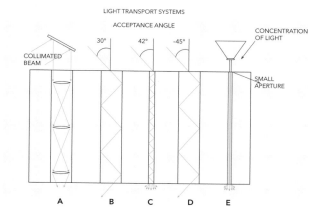

6.58

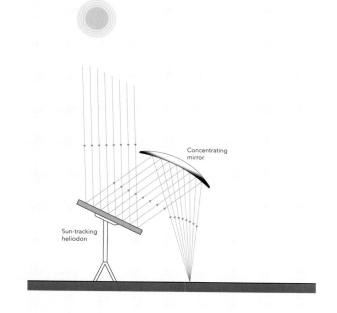

6.59

6.57 – Light transport systems in a daylight-pipe (Courtesy: Ian Edmonds)

6.58 – The polycarbonate dome collects daylight and the highly reflective tube going through the attic of a building transports light downward by inter-reflections (photo: M. Boubekri)

6.59 – A sun-tracking heliostat with a concentrating mirror

Figures 6.61 and 6.62 depict the exponential relationships between the efficiency of a tubular lightpipe and its aspect ratio from two different empirical measurements.

Hollow tubular lightpipes, made by Monodraught Ltd. were used in the Copper Box Olympic sports arena in London, United Kingdom, used during the 2012 London Olympic Games 6.63-6.65. The architect, Make Architects, specified a system that could deliver a 4% daylight factor on the floor of the arena. Working with ARUP, the consulting engineer, Monodraught provided a hollow lightpipe system that included 88 total 1500mm diameter lightpipes positioned strategically above the field of play delivering the required daylight levels as specified by the architect.

Hollow tubular lightpipes channel light in a vertical or horizontal direction. They also may change directions to avoid obstacles within a building structure. Changes in direction of the lightpipe duct create bends and elbows that increase friction and internal-reflections, causing additional light losses approximating 14% of loss in efficiency for each bend (Oakley et al., 2000). The extent of the loss in efficiency is relative to the bend angle and the length of the bend (Carter, 2002). It is possible to lose more than 14% and perhaps as much as 25% for each bend for the length of a bend equal to the diameter of the pipe due to inter-reflections occurring within each bend 6.66.

As a way to augment solar collection, laser cut panels may be used in conjunction with hollow mirror lightpipes to bend the incoming light and direct it down the pipe within a desired acceptance angle 6.67. A 2m diameter hollow mirror lightpipe with an aspect ratio of 9.1, covered with a pyramidal structure made of laser cut clear acrylic panels, produced substantial daylight levels at each of the eight floors that the lightpipe served (Garcia-Hansen and Edmonds, 2003). The extraction mechanism in this case was a cone-shaped reflecting device coupled with a horizontal shelf to deflect light upward onto a celling in order to minimize glare 6.68. With a 45° extraction cone, the measured illuminance ranged from 50 lux to 200 lux at each floor. With a 35° extraction cone, light levels were even higher, ranging between 50 lux and 400 lux.

6.60a

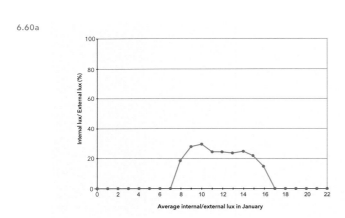

6.60b

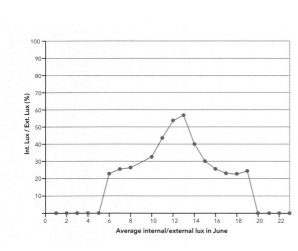

6.61

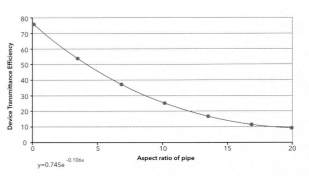

$$y = 0.745e^{-0.106x}$$

6.62

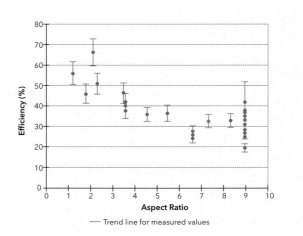

— Trend line for measured values

6.63

6.64

6.65

6.60a–b – Daylight penetration factor in January (a) and June (b) (Courtesy: © J. Callow)

6.61 – Relationship between efficiency and the aspect ratio of a tubular lightpipe with 99% inside reflectance (Courtesy: © Sage Publications)

6.62 – Relationship between efficiency and the aspect ratio of a tubular lightpipe with 95% inside reflectance (Courtesy: © Sage Publications)

6.63 – 1500mm-diameter Monodraught lightpipes of the Copper Box Olympic Arena, London, United Kingdom (Photo courtesy: © Monodraught Ltd.)

6.64 – Solar collection mechanism of lightpipes used in the Copper Box Olympic Arena (Photo courtesy: © Monodraught Ltd.)

6.65 – 88 Monodraught light-pipes deliver a minimum day-light factor of 4% on the floor of the Copper Box Olympic Arena (Photo courtesy: © Monodraught Ltd.)

6.66 – Graph of efficiency against bend angle for bend length equal to pipe diameter (Courtesy: © Sage Publications)

6.67 – Laser cut panels deflect sunlight down a lightpipe (Courtesy: Ian Edmonds)

6.66

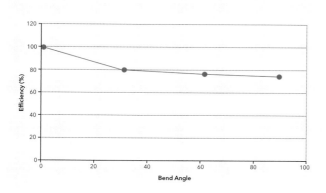

6.67

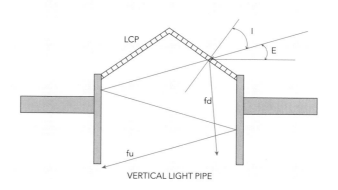

Mirrors and Lenses

An arrangement of mirrors and lenses also may be used to collect and redirect light down a shaft where lenses can help channel light downward by focusing and collimating light. Such systems could achieve efficiency of up to 28% after passing through 13 lenses (Smith, 2004). Mirrors and lenses were used in a lightpipe installed to transport sunlight to an underground research office located 33m below ground on the campus of the University of Minnesota 6.69. The system consisted of a solar tracking mirror housed in a glass room 6.70 and a simple shaft containing a series of optical lenses. The focusing lenses controlled the transport of light to the underground office and minimized the losses within the shaft. Figure 6.71 shows the sunlight delivered to the underground office 33m below ground.

Prism Light Guides

Lightpipe transport systems may be prism light guides, hollow structures with clear right-angled acrylic that transport light via internal reflections within the walls of the hollow prism guide 6.72. An example of a system using a glass prism can be found in the lightpipe designed by James Carpenter and Davidson Norris for the headquarters office of the Morgan Lewis Interna-tional Law Office 6.73-6.75. Inside the 14-story building is a 20m by 2.5m courtyard which rises over a height of 50m. The designers developed a 36m long light lightpipe, which extends from the atrium roof to approximately 4.5m above the courtyard level. The pipe has a double-skin construction, with an outer layer of synthetic-fiber fabric and a core made of glass prisms. The glass core is a conical shape with a diameter of 175cm at the top and 50cm at the bottom. An automated roof mounted heliostat tracks the sun and reflects light via a mirror into the glass core, where the prisms reflect the light downward 6.73.

Another prism light guide was used in the Canadian Telecommunications eight-story building near Toronto, Canada. The solar collection system consisted of eight solar tracking mirrors 6.76, each reflecting sunlight onto a solar concentrator that focuses light onto a smaller area of a prismatic guide that channel daylight inside the building. Infra-red and UV filters were applied to allow only a visible spectrum inside the building. The entire system was housed in a glass room to protect it from weather. The daylighting system was incorporated with the electric lighting strategy 6.77 in such a way that both daylighting and electric light were delivered through the same light extractor. 6.78

6.68

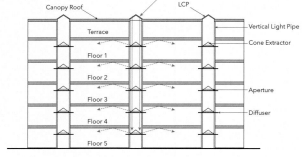

6.69

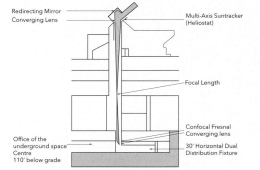

A Sunlighting system at the University of Minnesota. Tracking mirrors on the roof direct sunlight 33m below ground where it is used to illuminate an underground space.

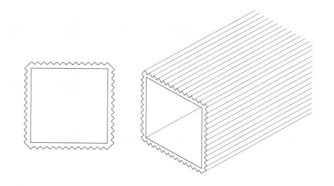

6.68 – Solar lightpipe directing light eight floors below with a cone-shaped light extracting system (Courtesy: Ian Edmonds)

6.69 – Solar lightpipe at the University of Minnesota, USA, directing light 33m below ground to an underground office

6.70 – A solar tracking mirror collects daylight and sends it through an opening in the roof of a building on the campus of the University of Minnesota, USA (Photo: M. Boubekri)

6.71 – Sunlight received 33m below ground in an underground research office on the campus of the University of Minnesota (Photo: M. Boubekri)

6.72 – Hollow prism light guide

6.73 – Lightpipe in Morgan Lewis Office, Washington, DC, USA, brings daylight down twelve stories (Photo courtesy: Morgan & Norris)

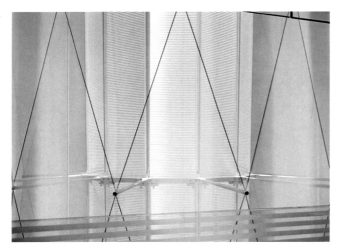

6.74 – Detail of the lightpipe in Morgan Lewis Office (Photo courtesy: Morgan & Norris)

6.75 – Heliostat above the Morgan Lewis Office (Photo courtesy: Morgan & Norris)

6.76 – Lightpipes made of eight sun tracking heliostats, eight concentrating mirrors, and eight hollow core prismatic guides are housed in a glass shed in an eight-story building in Toronto, Canada (Photo courtesy: TRI Systems Inc.)

6.77 – Daylight strategy well integrated within the electric lighting system of a multistory building using daylight pipe

6.78 – Daylight emitters well integrated within the electric lighting system of a multi-story building using daylight pipe to illuminate an eight-story building in Toronto, Canada (Photo courtesy: TRI Systems Inc.)

6.79 – The lightpipe of the Borusan Holdings Building in Istanbul, Turkey

6.80 – Sun tracking heliostat of the lightpipe of the Borusan Holdings Building (Photo: M. Boubekri)

Sunlight beamed from roof

Rotating Mirror (Solar Position)

(Lamp Position)

Piped light to interior

Collimating Optics

Metal Halide lamp with Reflector

Duct to HVAC System

STRATEGIES AND SYSTEMS PERFORMANCE

A vertical lightpipe with prismatic guide was also used in the Borusan Holdings Building in Istanbul, Turkey 6.79, 6.80. Borusan was seeking a means to increase the natural light within their building which operates during weekdays as an office building, and during weekends as a museum of high-tech modern arts. The overall length of the lightpipe is 8 meters outside and 24 meters inside with 80 cm in diameter. The lightpipe runs down across four floors. The installed Heliobus Light Pipe achieved significant daylight levels, as high as 400 lux in the upper floor and 150 lux on the lower floor on a sunny day according to the building manager 6.81.

Research has shown that prism light guides having aspect ratios of 30 could achieve efficiencies of nearly 30% (Aizenburg, 1997). As with most of these light transport mechanisms, efficiency depends on the angle of entry of the light, also known as the acceptance angle. For prism light guides with right angles, light must enter at an angle of 27.6° or less in order to maximize reflection.

A horizontal lightpipe system using prism guides as a distribution system was developed by SunCentral Inc., in Vancouver, Canada. The system has three main classes of components – a solar harvesting tracking system 6.82, a light transporting prism guide, and a light distribution system 6.83, 6.84. The collection system includes an array of small computer-controlled tracking square mirrors mounted on each floor above the windows along the outside wall of the building that has the greatest exposure to sunlight 6.82, 6.83. After being reflected from the mirror array, the collected sunlight is concentrated using Fresnel lenses and re-collimated by off-axis parabolic mirrors, then channeled through reflective tubes 6.84 to a central location. From the central location where light is concentrated, light is channeled inside the building through ducts containing a prismatic film that transport the light by internal reflections until it is distributed inside the room. The duct may be located within the ceiling cavity such as the system used in the British Columbia

6.78

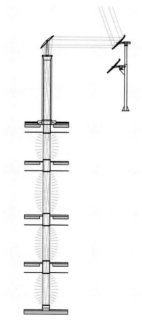
6.79

6.80

6.81

6.83

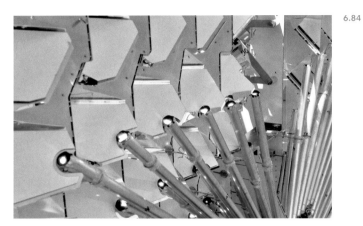

6.84

6.82

6.81 – Prismatic guide of the lightpipe of the Borusan Holdings Building (Photo: M. Boubekri)

6.82 – Solar tracking collectors of a horizontal lightpipe at the Biological Sciences Building at the University of British Columbia, Vancouver, Canada (Photo courtesy: © SunCentral Inc.)

6.83 – Prototype of the British Columbia Institute of Technology, solar collector using concentrating Fresnel lenses, Vancouver, Canada (Photo courtesy: © SunCentral Inc.)

6.84 – Prototype of the British Columbia Institute of Technology solar collector using concentrating Fresnel lenses and reflective tubes (Photo courtesy: © SunCentral Inc.)

6.85 – Inside of the original version of the British Columbia Institute of Technology solar collector integrated with electric lighting system (Photo courtesy: © SunCentral Inc.)

6.86 – Linear lightpipe with ceiling integrated light distribution system at the British Columbia Institute of Technology (Photo courtesy: © SunCentral Inc.)

6.87 – Linear lightpipe with exposed light distribution system, in the Department of Biological Sciences Building at the University of British Columbia (Photo: M. Boubekri)

Institute of Technology (BCIT) 6.85 or as linear light fixtures 6.86, 6.87, such as the system used in the Biological Sciences Building at the University of British Columbia (UBC). The light transport system consists of prismatic guides that are integrated with LED electric lamps. Data provided by the manufacturer of these horizontal lightpipes, SunCentral Inc., suggests that the system used in the BCIT provides approximately 500 peak lux of daylight and the system used at the UBC delivers about 700 peak lux (measured at the task plane, approximately 90cm from the ground). According to data on the SunCentral Inc. web site, British Columbia Hydro, the leading electric utility in British Columbia, has conducted an in-depth study of the installation at the British Columbia Institute of Technology. The energy saved by using this system was 50% in peak daily power, 42% in summer monthly average power savings, and 36.5% in annual average power savings.

6.85

6.86

6.87

Fiber Optics

Fiber optics transport light totally by internal reflection within the "walls" of the fiber. Fibers usually are made of silicate glass or plastic. Plastic fibers afford a tremendous advantage of flexibility and convenience which allows them to channel light just about anywhere. But bundled optical fibers large enough to be used for daylighting applications would be too heavy and too costly. Due to their small cross section, fiber optics needs to be coupled with a sunlight concentrating device to increase efficiency. Examples of such applications are the systems commercialized by such companies as Parans in Sweden 6.88, 6.89 and Sunlight Direct in the United States 6.90, 6.91. An array of optical lenses encapsulated within a roof-mounted solar heliostat tracks sunlight and transmits it through fiber optics. Light may be channeled to different portions of the building. Figure 6.92, provided by Sunlight Direct™, depicts the performance of the Sunlight Direct fiber optics lightpipes.

6.88

6.89

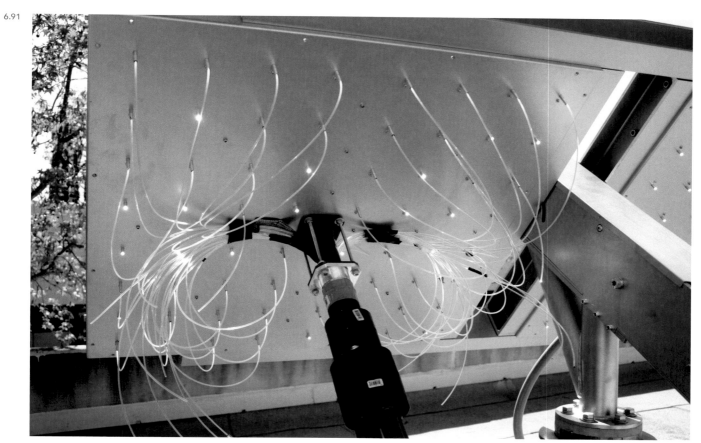

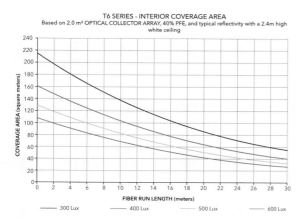

T6 SERIES - INTERIOR COVERAGE AREA
Based on 2.0 m² OPTICAL COLLECTOR ARRAY, 40% PFE, and typical reflectivity with a 2.4m high white ceiling

COVERAGE AREA (square meters)

FIBER RUN LENGTH (meters)

—— 300 Lux   —— 400 Lux   —— 500 Lux   —— 600 Lux

6.88 – Solar collectors made by Parans (Photo courtesy: © Parans)

6.89 – Solar lighting with fiber optics in a hospital in Sweden (Photo courtesy: © Parans)

6.90 – Sunlight Direct solar trackers with Fresnel lenses concentrating light onto a fiber optics entryway (Photo: M. Boubekri)

6.91 – Fiber optics light transport mechanism of the Sunlight Direct System (Photo: M. Boubekri)

6.92 – Performance of fiber optic lightpipe system of Sunlight Direct (Courtesy: © Sunlight Direct Inc.)

CHAPTER 7

CASE STUDIES

ST Diamond Building
Putrajaya (near Kuala Lumpur), Malaysia

Research Support Facility at the National Renewable Energy Laboratory
Golden, Colorado, USA

Augsburg City Library
Augsburg, Germany

TNT Centre
Hoofddorp, the Netherlands

Asian Development Bank Headquarters
Manila, Philippines

Adidas Laces
Herzogenaurach, Germany

Lewis Integrative Science Building
University of Oregon, Eugene, Oregon, USA

Changi Airport Terminal 3
Singapore

Extension of the High Museum of Art
Atlanta, Georgia, USA

Extension of the Art Institute of Chicago
Chicago, Illinois, USA

Sino-Italian Ecological and Energy Efficient Building
Tsinghua University, Beijing, China

Cathedral of Christ the Light
Oakland, California, USA

Schlaues Haus
Oldenburg, Germany

CASE STUDIES

ST Diamond Building

Putrajaya (near Kuala Lumpur), Malaysia

Year: 2010 **Architect:** NR Architect & NR Interior Design **MEP Engineer:** Primetech Sdn Bhd **Daylighting Consultants:** IEN Consultants Sdn Bhd **Primary Daylighting Strategy:** A four-sided atrium supplies the building core with daylight from the top. Mirrored lightshelves and mirrored louvers supply and control daylight from the sides of the building.

1 – Atrium viewed from the ground floor of the ST Diamond Building, Putrajaya, Malaysia (Photo courtesy: Energy Commission Malaysia)
2 – Self-shading inverted pyramidal shape (Photo courtesy: Energy Commission Malaysia)

The headquarters building of the Malaysian Energy Commission, known as the ST Diamond Building, was completed in 2009 and occupied since June 2010. Designed to be an innovative building in its architecture and sustainable concept, this seven-story building, with a self-shading inverted pyramid slanted at a 25° angle from horizontal, protects itself during the hot hours of the day 1. In doing so its exposure to the sun from the east and west is minimized in the country's blazing hot climate. Interior spaces are organized around a top lit atrium that brings in daylight to the core area of the building 2-6. To this day, it is the first and only building in Malaysia to be certified with the Platinum Green Building Index – the highest certification level in Malaysia. The building is topped with photovoltaic (PV) solar panels which generate about 10% of the building's electrical energy 7.

2

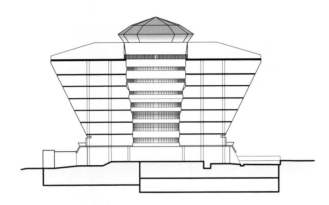

3 – A light deflecting mirror on the fourth floor provides daylight down the atrium, and lightshelves deflect sunlight from the building perimeter to the core areas (Photo courtesy: IEN Consultants)

4 – Section through the atrium

5 – Atrium viewed from the top floor

6 – Daylight levels at the ground level of the atrium

(Photo courtesy: Energy Commission Malaysia)

7 – PV panels on the roof provide 10% of the electricity needs (Photo courtesy: Energy Commission Malaysia)

8 – Mirror lightshelf with 30° tilt angle (Photo courtesy: Energy Commission Malaysia)

Building Performance

The mirrored lightshelf design with fixed reflective louvers and large window stools allows diffuse daylight inside the peripheral area of the building while reducing glare [8]. The ST Diamond Building incorporates an atrium within its core with windows of the adjacent rooms increasing in size from top to bottom, allowing more daylight to penetrate the rooms located on the lower floors of the atrium. The atrium daylighting system incorporates a dome with automatically controlled blinds that can take six different positions to maintain stable daylight levels in the atrium and reduce glare from direct sunlight. Semi-specular atrium wall panels slanted at an angle of 10° from the vertical help to reflect light across the atrium to the lowest two levels 1 and 2 where daylight intensities are lowest. Windows around the atrium increase in size from top to bottom according to daylight availability inside the atrium, with the largest windows at the bottom of the atrium. Reflective panels on the top floors, tilted at 10°, help reflect light to the first and second floors.

The inverted pyramidal shape of the building allows larger floor plates at the top which are more exposed to daylight from the atrium side as well as the exterior side. Smaller floor plates are at the bottom with a small building footprint for more landscaping opportunity. The results of these strategies are such that 20% of the floor area is daylit by the atrium and 30% is daylit by the outer envelope. The inverted-pyramid as a self-shading strategy has proven to be a very effective passive energy saving strategy allowing the building to reduce significantly solar heat gains especially in hot tropical climates such as Malaysia [10].

The mirror lightshelf and the atrium as daylighting strategies allow a daylight coverage of 5m from facade and 2m for circulation space in the middle of the office [11]. The ST Diamond Building has a building energy index of 69 kWh/m^2 per year (without photovoltaics), and 56kWh/m^2 per year (with photovoltaics), which is roughly the third of typical office buildings of similar size and cooling capacity in Malaysia. According to the energy consultant, lights are not on 50% of the time and lighting savings are about 77% compared to the Green Mark base which uses a reference building considered to be a typical office building in the country. The building also incorporates a roof daylighting system with a south facing opening that takes in diffuse light from the sky. The light painted walls and the grillage deflect daylight softly into the space below, which is a seating area for informal gatherings or reading [12].

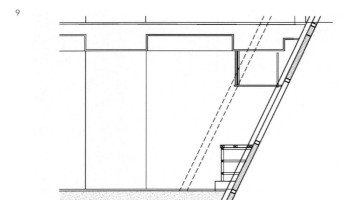

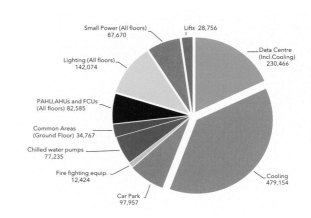

Small Power (All floors) 87,670
Lifts 28,756
Data Centre (Incl.Cooling) 230,466
Lighting (All floors) 142,074
PAHU,AHUs and FCUs (All floors) 82,585
Common Areas (Ground Floor) 34,767
Chilled water pumps 77,235
Fire fighting equip. 12,424
Car Park 97,957
Cooling 479,154

9 – Detailed section view of the lightshelf system and window stool (Photo courtesy: IEN Consultants)

10 – ST Diamond Building measured energy consumption for the 2011 year (Kwh/Year) (Photo courtesy: IEN Consultants)

11 – Large window sills act as a second lightshelf (Photo courtesy: Energy Commission Malaysia)

12 – Seating area with daylight coming through the roof lighting system (Photo courtesy: Energy Commission Malaysia)

CASE STUDIES

Research Support Facility at the National Renewable Energy Laboratory

Golden, Colorado, USA

Year: 2010 **Architecture, Interiors, Landscape Design, and Lighting:** RNL Design **General Contractor:** Haselden Construction **MEP Engineers:** Stantec **Energy, Daylighting, and Sustainable Design Consultant** (including LEED Certification process management): Architectural Energy Corporation **Primary Daylighting Strategy:** Sidelighting with special louver system (LightLouver™ Daylighting System), floor to ceiling height of approx. 4m and floor plate depth of approx. 18m.

The Research Support Facility (RSF) is a 20,400m² federal office building designed to accommodate 822 occupants and to serve as an example of a net-zero energy, environmentally responsive building. The building is organized into a three-story wing and a four-story wing, each oriented along an east-west axis, with a connecting entry and a conference and service core element. Construction cost was US $57.4 million [2, 3].

Overall project's goals included the following:
- meet all functional and safety requirements
- net-zero energy use, with annual energy consumption of 79 kWh/m² or less prior to any renewable energy contribution
- platinum LEED certification
- flexibility and expandability to accommodate reconfiguration of office areas and expansion of the facility.

1 - Interior of top floor of south wing – LightLouver™ units of the Research Support Facility at the National Renewable Energy Laboratory in Golden, Colorado, USA, in the upper portion of the punched windows on the right side of the image, and north facing view and daylight windows on the left side of the image (Photo courtesy: Light-Louver™)

2 - Plan view (Photo courtesy: LightLouver™)

3 - Aerial view (Photo courtesy: LightLouver™)

2

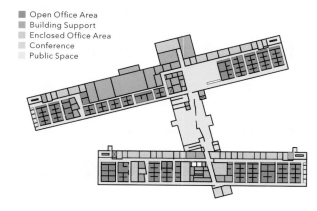

■ Open Office Area
■ Building Support
■ Enclosed Office Area
■ Conference
■ Public Space

3

Building Performance

A primary architectural and energy design strategy was daylighting the entire office floor plate. As a consequence, the floor plate width was limited to approximately 18m, and the floor to ceiling clearance was increased from the typical 2.5m ceiling to approximately 4m. This approach resulted in two long, thin multi-story wings oriented along an east-west axis and connected by a central element that housed the entry, conference rooms, and a service core. The thin high floor plate allow for deep daylight distribution, cross ventilation from the operable windows, and thermal stratification from the under floor ventilation system.

Two side-daylighting strategies were employed to daylight the entire office floor plate. The first was a passive optical side-daylighting system, the LightLouver™ 1, 6, 7, a daylighting system which uses patented reflective slats to collect and redirect sunlight onto the ceiling and deep into the interior space. The Light-Louver™ units, measuring 1.59m wide by 91.5cm high, are located in the "daylight windows," above the "vision windows" in the punched window openings of the Thermomass™ exterior wall panels. The LightLouver™ units have been sized to redirect sunlight more than approximately 13.5m deep into the building to wash sunlight across the white office ceiling where it is reflected to the space below. When the sunlight provided by the Light-Louver™ units is combined with daylight from the north facing windows, a fully daylit floor plate is achieved.

The second side-daylighting strategy was north facing windows positioned low for views and high for deeper daylight penetration. Daylight harvesting (the ability to turn off or dim the electric lights in the presence of adequate daylight) is accomplished by a closed loop electric lighting control system consisting of a number of photosensors connected to each row (circuit) of electric pendant lighting fixtures. When adequate lighting is provided at the working surface (75cm above the finished floor), the electric lights turn off or dim as necessary to ensure that adequate ambient lighting is provided while maximizing energy savings.

Figures 4 and 5 present plots which highlight the predicted and measured performance of the RSF lighting system. The first figure is a series of plots indicating the lighting power of the RSF for a few days in September 2010. One plot shows the measured power of the electric lighting in the RSF while a second plot indicates the installed lighting power at the RSF; the third plot indicates the baseline lighting power allowed by the ASHRAE/IES 90.1 Energy Efficiency Standard. It is clear from this figure that the RSF is using substantially less power for lighting than either the installed total lighting power or the allowed lighting power, on the order of 85% savings compared to the allowed lighting power usage and 75% compared to the installed lighting power.

The second figure presents a series of average monthly lighting power density plots for the period December 2010 to November 2011. The daytime average lighting power density is on the order of 1.66 to 2.22W/m². This is 85% below the ASHRAE/IES 90.1 required level of 11 W/m², indicating that the RSF daylighting systems, in combination with effective and properly operating lighting controls, are functioning and performing extremely well, and deliver the anticipated ambient illumination and the predicted energy savings.

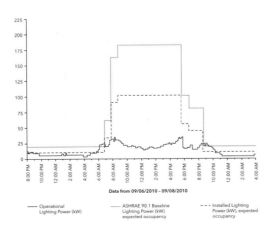

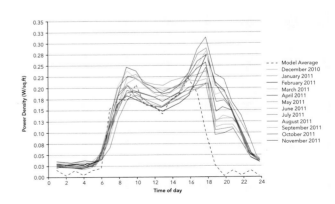

4 – Plot of average measured electric lighting power profile for a few days compared to ASHRAE/IES 90.1 baseline lighting power consumption and installed lighting power consumption (Photo courtesy: LightLouver™)

5 – Plot of average monthly measured lighting power density compared to modeled average monthly lighting power density (Photo courtesy: LightLouver™)

6 – Section detail of the LightLouver system

7 – South facade (Photo courtesy: LightLouver™)

8 – South facade of three-story south wing – "Daylight Windows" with LightLouver™ units located above the "Vision Windows," which are surrounded by a shadow-box to reduce solar heat gain into the building (Photo courtesy: LightLouver™)

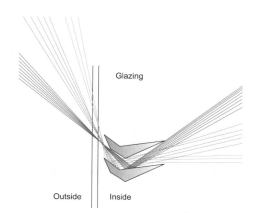

Glazing

Outside   Inside

Augsburg
City Library

Augsburg, Germany

Year: 2009 **Architect:** Schrammel Architekten
General Contractor: Wohnungsbaugesellschaft
der Stadt Augsburg **Energy, Daylighting, and
Sustainable Design Consultant:** Light Trumpets,
Bartenbach GmbH, Aldrans / Innsbruck **Primary
Daylighting Strategy:** Mirror toplighting system

1 – Interior view of the Augsburg
City Library, Augsburg, Germany
(Photo courtesy: Schrammel
Architekten)
2 – Exterior view (Photo courtesy:
Bartenbach GmbH, © Peter Barten-
bach)

Located in the middle of the historic city, the library
that features "open architecture" provides transparency
for the people. A skylight of 400 mirrors directs light
into the heart of the structure. Colorful interior design,
colorful vertical shading devices, and double-skin glazing on the sides complement this effort for natural light.
The building exterior is a strikingly modern building in
the historic district of Augsburg 2.

The new City Library in Augsburg was designed
according to the concept of "Open Book – Open House"
1, 3-5. The architectural concept envisaged a transparent
structure with large glass facades in order to achieve
a high level of comfort and a high ecological standard
with an innovative energy concept. The architectural and
energy concept was integrated through careful planning
of architectural and building systems during the early
stages of the design. New City Library shows a strong
emphasis for sustainable design due to very low power
consumption of primary energy and on the wellbeing of
the building occupants.

2

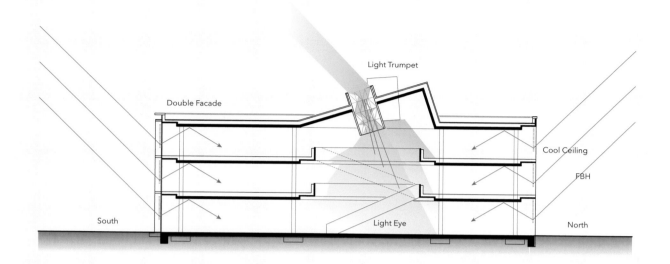

Light Trumpet

Double Facade

Cool Ceiling

FBH

South

Light Eye

North

3 – Interior view (Photo courtesy: Schrammel Architekten)

4 – Interior view (Photo courtesy: Bartenbach GmbH, © Peter Bartenbach)

5 – Central of the library (Photo courtesy: Schrammel Architekten)

6 – Section showing the light trumpets and the ventilation system (Courtesy: Schrammel Architekten)

7 – Close-up view of one of the four light trumpets (Photo courtesy: Detlef Schobert)

8 – Close-up view of one of the four light trumpets (Photo courtesy: Schrammel Architekten)

Building Performance

In the areas illuminated from the top, there are three so-called "light trumpets" – specially developed light shafts clad with high gloss, specular aluminium reaching from the roof downward through three levels of the building 6-8. The distinctive feature inside the light shaft comprises more than 400 precisely shaped faceted mirrors reflecting daylight in the center of the building, providing adequate general lighting through the day. When the sun shines, the ever changing sun patterns around the stairway add life and excitement to the core of the building.

Light redirecting louvers made of automatically controlled, highly specular aluminium mounted to the facades provide effective sun protection while channeling daylight into the building from the sides 9, 10.

The louver angles change position depending on the position of the sun. Reflective ceiling panels transport natural light further into the depth of the interior spaces. As a result, the book stacks area and the reading zones are well illuminated with uniform and glare-free daylight. A daylight factor of 3% has been achieved according to the daylighting consultant in this project, Bartenbach GmbH.

The artificial lighting in this building serves solely as a supplement to daylight. During the daytime, the electric lighting system is usually off. This building is highly automated. The amount of daylight entering the building is controlled by a central control system (building automation). Due to the daylighting concept, the overall energy consumption of the building could be reduced to an extremely low maximum value of 126 kWh/m² per annum, achieving nearly 50% reduction of energy consumption from daylighting alone.

9

9 – Photo showing daylight penetration from reflective louvers and "light trumpets" (Photo courtesy: Schrammel Architekten)

10 – Reflective aluminium louvers redirect light deep into the library (Photo courtesy: Bartenbach GmbH, © Peter Bartenbach)

TNT Centre

Hoofddorp, the Netherlands

Year: 2011 **Architect:** Paul de Ruiter
Client: Triodos-OVG Green Offices B.V. **MEP**
Engineer: DGMR en B & R Adviseurs voor
Duurzaamheid **Primary Daylighting Strategy:**
Atrium, louver system

TNT Centre houses the TNR Group, a global express delivery service provider from the Netherlands. This project, completed in March 2011, enjoys the status of being the first Platinum LEED rated building in Europe [2,3]. It provides space for nearly 900 employees. The management and employees of the TNT group adopted a new model of working called "working unplugged" where employees are free to decide their optimum working locations and schedules. This model has far-reaching consequences for the building and its exploitation, allowing TNT to save nearly 40% of the normal space requirement with a much higher efficiency of use of the building. The guiding principle in the design of the TNT Centre is "connectivity," where the user of the building is key. According to the architect, this principle translated into an open and transparent building that comprises a U-shaped six-floor main volume around an atrium. This atrium is the heart of the building and serves as a single large meeting area [1].

1 – Multi-terraced three-sided atrium of the TNT Centre, Hoofddorp, the Netherlands (Photo courtesy: Paul de Ruiter Architects)

2 – Exterior view (Photo courtesy: Paul de Ruiter Architects)

2

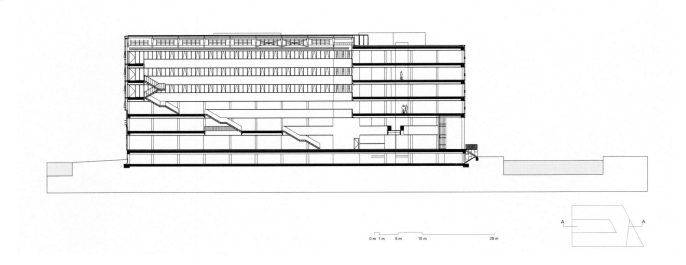

0 m 1 m   5 m   10 m   25 m

A———————A

Building Performance

Daylighting was a major design consideration in the TNT Centre and the leitmotif in the design of the building, not only for energy consideration but also for the users' health and well-being. The six-story building is centered around a three-sided atrium, whereby daylight enters the core of the building from the roof and from one side of the atrium. Offices are located directly around the atrium, allowing daylight to enter the adjacent work spaces 5, 7. The building has a completely glazed north facade. Aluminium Window System (AWS 102 and AWS 65) were used with respective visible transmittance of 0.5 and 0.6, allowing for an extensive low U-value glazing of 1.4 W/(m² °K) (Zeller, 2011). Smart innovative sun blinds optimize daylight access from the south side of the building and provide shading and reduce cooling loads during the summer.

All the measures taken to reduce the heat, lighting, and cooling loads resulted in low energy consumption. The building power consumption is 28 W/m²; 20 W/m² due to occupants and equipment. Electric lighting consumed only lighting 8 W/m². Energy savings strategies utilized on site allowed the TNT Centre to have very low energy consumption. The Centre uses 9.8kWh/m²/year for heating and 3.3kWh/m²/year for cooling (Zeller, 2012).

3 – Exterior south facade (Photo courtesy: Paul de Ruiter Architects)

4 – Open plan favors the concept of connectivity intended (Photo courtesy: Paul de Ruiter Architects)

5 – Offices adjacent to the atrium benefit from the daylight within (Photo courtesy: Paul de Ruiter Architects)

6 – Longitudinal section across the three-sided atrium (Courtesy: Paul de Ruiter Architects)

7 – Three-sided atrium (Photo courtesy: Paul de Ruiter Architects)

7

Asian Development Bank Headquarters

Manila, Philippines

Year: 2003-2006 **Architect/ Principal Consultant:** Dr. Nima Kishnan **Client:** Asian Development Bank **MEP Engineer:** CPGreen & Cpg Cnsultants Pte Ltd **Daylighting Consultants:** IEN Consultants, Khun Thida Kyaw **Primary Daylighting Strategy:** Atrium, large light-deflecting mirrors

1 – Retrofitted roof cover viewed from inside of the Asia Development Bank Head-quarters Building in Manila, Philippines (Photo courtesy: Asian Development Bank)
2 – Exterior view (Photo courtesy: Asian Development Bank)

The Asian Development Bank was built in the 1980s. It is a large office building with a deep floor plate in which some employees have offices adjacent to the two atria in the building. The atria, measuring 30m x 30m, are nine stories high and are capped by a pyramidal roof with a central skylight and continuous clerestories all around 2. The original design incorporated a dense screen under the skylight that filtered much of the sunlight and prevented it from entering the atrium. Daylight levels, measured during sunny days at the ground floor of the atrium, which constitutes a library, were no more than 100 lux. As a result, electric lighting was needed practically at all times on the atrium floor 3, 4.

The Asian Development Bank decided to retrofit this building in a direct response to expressed occupant discomfort. Many of the users' complaints were about lack of daylight. CPGreen was commissioned to study the problem of insufficient natural light, an environmental condition that seemed to adversely affect staff morale and comfort. The building retrofit commenced in 2003 and was completed in 2006.

2

6

3 – Roof condition and lighting in the atrium before retrofit (Photo courtesy: Asian Development Bank)

4 – Lighting in atrium before retrofit (Photo courtesy: Asian Development Bank)

5 & 6 – Large mirrors placed around the atrium skylight deflect daylight inside the atrium (Photo courtesy: Asian Development Bank)

7 – Large reflecting mirror around the atrium roof structure (Photo courtesy: Asian Development Bank)

Building Performance

This retrofit project was unique in that it used the daylighting strategy of one of largest reflecting mirrors in Asia. Due to numerous concerns related to typhoons, hot weather, etc., the solution was designed to increase daylight penetration inside the atrium without puncturing the existing roof structure. The final solution was to install very large reflective mirrors around the outside perimeter of the clerestories 1, 5-7. The mirrors harvest the incident sunlight and redirect it inside the atrium. The criteria estab-

lished included maximizing daylight inside the atrium with the condition that no direct sunlight would cause glare for adjacent office workers. To achieve this goal, the mirrors were constructed from polished aluminium sheets that reflect the incoming sunlight as a gentle watery pattern inside the two atria 9, 10. The existing grillage below the skylight was modified to contain larger openings allowing more daylight inside the atrium. Onsite measurements of daylight showed daylight levels six times higher than before retrofit under sunny conditions, and four times higher under overcast sky conditions. At the atrium floor, illuminance levels of 300 lux were measured 75% of the time during business hours (Reimann, 2010) 8, 11.

8 – Daylight inside the atrium after retrofit (Photo courtesy: Asian Development Bank)

9 – Inside the atrium after retrofit (Photo courtesy: Asian Development Bank)

10 – The top of atrium after retrofit viewed from an adjacent interior corridor (Photo courtesy: Asian Development Bank)

11 – Daylight on the floor of the atrium after retrofit (Photo courtesy: Asian Development ment Bank)

8

9

Adidas Laces

Herzogenaurach, Germany

Year: 2011 **Architect:** kadawittfeldarchitektur, Germany **Project Partner:** Dirk Zweering **Client:** Adidas Ag. World of Sports **General Contractor:** Max Bögl **MEP Engineer:** Planungsgruppe m+m, böblingen in coop. with jürgensen+baumgartner, Pliezhausen in coop. with Bartenbach GmbH, Aldrans / Innsbruck **Daylighting Consultant:** Bartenbach GmbH **Primary Daylighting Strategy:** Core Atrium

1 – Interior bridges and inner glass walls of offices adjacent the atrium of the Adidas Laces Corporate Building in Herzogenaurach, Germany (Photo courtesy: Bartenbach GmbH; © Werner Huthmacher)

2 – Ground floor plan
3 – Exterior view (Photo courtesy: Bartenbach GmbH; © Werner Huthmacher)

2

Floorplan Office Module
1 Flexible Office Spaces
2 "Laces"
3 Office Lounge
4 Air Space

The Adidas Laces project is a 2009 award winning project for "Best Innovative Concept" designed by the German architectural firm kadawittfeldarchitektur. The construction was completed and the building occupied in 2011. This five-story structure is a research and development facility for the athletic brand Adidas World of Sports that provides 1700 workstations 2, 3. The building footprint follows a zigzag shape formation. Organized in a circular arrangement, all the workstations housed in this building are interconnected across a 500 m² central atrium with a series of elevated crisscrossing bridges giving the name of "laces" to the building 1, 4, 5. These bridges span a maximum distance of 50 meters. These interconnecting pathways allow employees to communicate easily and efficiently. All office areas are flanked with large glazed inner glass walls and large windows on the exterior enjoying high-quality daylighting 6, 7. The atrium is covered with ETFE (Ethylene tetrafluoroethylene) lightweight, 4-meter-wide cushion panels with length varying between 35 and 50 m supported by slender arches that span the entire width of the atrium 8-10.

The outer facade consists of a highly insulated three-layer structural glazing construction that complies with German standards in respect to thermal and moisture protection. The ETFE atrium cover provides high corrosion resistance and strength over a wide temperature range. ETFE has a very high melting temperature, as well as excellent chemical, electrical, and thermal resistance properties.

3

Building
Performance

According to the architect, "Laces" exceeds the requirements of the German Directive on Energy Saving (EnEV) by 38.8%. The climate conditioning of the atrium is carried out by streaming conditioned air from the office areas using high air pressure such that no additional air conditioning costs are incurred to heat or cool the atrium space. Twenty-eight geothermal probes with a length of approximately 4300 meters result in 80 tons of CO_2 saved annually.

The use of smart daylight photosensors and dimmers allows substantial energy savings according to the building managers. The illumination of the "laces" in the whole atrium is supplied by means of a 750-meter-long LED lighting strip. An average daylight factor of 11% is achieved in the center of the atrium as measured by the author.

8

8 – ETFE roof cover with
arched aluminium structure
(Photo courtesy: Bartenbach
GmbH; © Werner Huthmacher)

9 – Exterior view of the ETFE
roof cover (Photo courtesy:
Bartenbach GmbH; © Werner
Huthmacher)

10 – Aerial view (Photo
courtesy: Bartenbach GmbH;
© Werner Huthmacher)

1

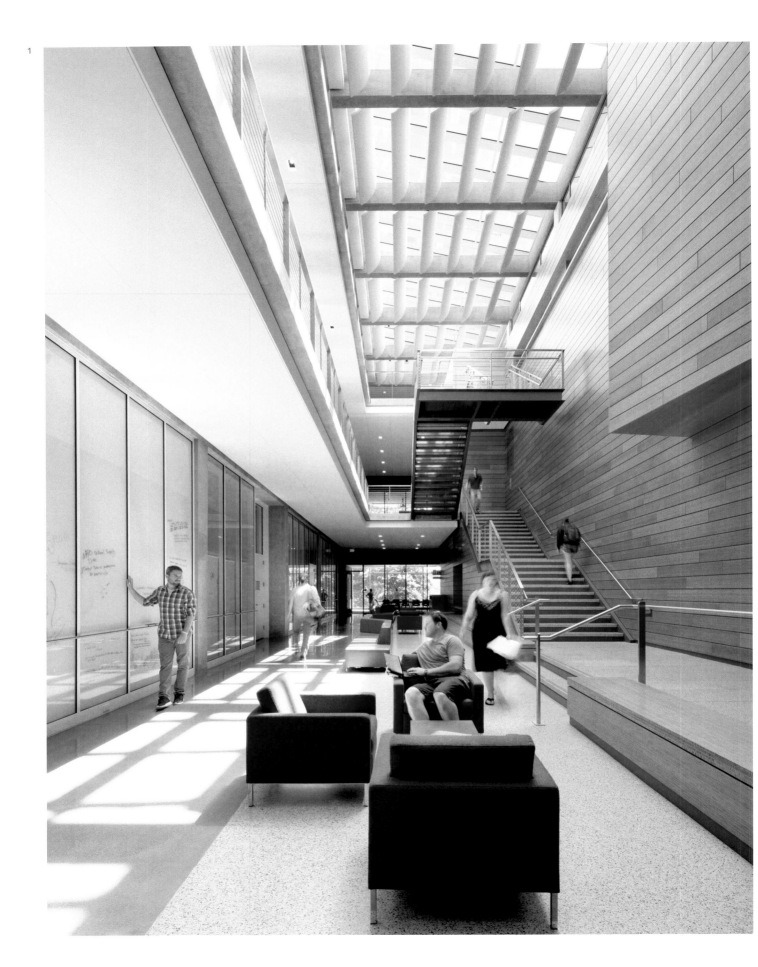

Lewis Integrative Science Building

University of Oregon, Eugene, Oregon, USA

Year: 2012 **Architect:** HDR Architecture & THA Architecture **Client:** University of Oregon, USA **MEP & Structural Engineering:** BHE Engineers and HDR/THA Architecture, Catena Engineers **Daylighting Consultant:** HDR Architecture & THA Architecture **Primary Daylighting Strategy:** Atrium, exterior, and lightshelves

1 – The atrium of the Lewis Integrative Science Building in Oregon, USA (Photo courtesy of HDR/THA Architecture; © 2013 Lara Swimmer)

The new Lewis Integrative Science Building (LISB) at the University of Oregon (UO) is a 10,300 m² building, home to research clusters centered around interdisciplinary and integrative research missions, where the majority of the space is devoted to studying the brain and its functions. The LISB is the newest addition to the university's Lorry I. Lokey Science Complex comprised of 12 buildings on the University of Oregon campus. The building consists of four occupied stories and an occupied subterranean level. Dispersed throughout the building are 46 offices, 10 collaborative meeting areas, and more than 3,000 m² of laboratory space.

The exterior design of the building embraces the architectural language found on the campus, influenced by the historic collection of brick buildings designed by Ellis F. Lawrence, one of the founders of the university's School of Architecture and Allied Arts 2. The first three floors of the exterior are composed of brick with precast concrete details. Expansive glass windows punch through the brick, with the south-facing windows shielded by sunshades and lightshelves. The fourth floor is enclosed completely with glass 4.

The building's main entrance opens to the south and is distinguished by its extensive use of glass 3. The transparency provides to users a preview into the dramatic three-story interior atrium. The interior architecture concept is based on the idea of connectivity and openness. The atrium constitutes the building's center of activity and collaboration 1. The atrium's materials are simple and reflect the architecture of the building – bamboo brings in warmth, and extensive use of glass allows science to be displayed and provides transparency into the working labs 6. Exterior and interior lightshelves are used in offices along peripheral walls for sunlight control and improved daylight distribution inside 5.

The atrium's expansive skylight harvests natural light deep into the core of the building and adjacent spaces. A layer of curved light-diffusing baffles 7 defines the skylight area and distributes daylight throughout the atrium and into neighboring offices. Rigorous testing of the skylight size, its location, and the design of its diffusers informed the final design of the skylight and atrium. This approach resulted in an atrium that needs little to no artificial light during the day and provides a warm and welcoming space for collaboration.

2 – Exterior view (Photo courtesy of HDR/THA Architecture; © 2013 Lara Swimmer)

3 – South entrance (Photo courtesy of HDR/THA Architecture; © 2013 Lara Swimmer)

4 – Punched windows in brick walls covered with lightshelves (Photo courtesy of HDR/THA Architecture; © 2013 Lara Swimmer)

5 – Interior lightshelves to control sunlight and improve daylight inside offices located along peripheral walls (Photo courtesy of HDR/THA Architecture; © 2013 Lara Swimmer)

Building Performance

LISB was modeled to achieve energy cost savings 60% above the U.S. National Energy Code (ASHRAE 90.1) and use 58% less energy than conventionally designed buildings of similar size and function. The most dramatic energy savings – approximately 17% – comes from extracting waste heat from a utility tunnel below the site and using the heat to control temperature in laboratories and office spaces.

The use of baffles in the top cover of the atrium allows careful control of sunlight inside the atrium in order to minimize overheating and glare problems. In addition to daylight admitted through the atrium to the core areas of the LISB, energy savings are also accomplished by placing window openings throughout the building to admit controlled daylight and reduce electric lighting use. Every window – from its size, depth of opening, and sunshade position – was influenced by sustainable research and daylight analyses. The ratio of opaque exterior walls to window areas carefully balances the goals of a tight building envelope and good daylighting. Measured daylight factor levels inside the atrium range between 3% and 8%.

Among many other sustainable design features the LISB enjoys are the following:

- daylight sensors and occupancy sensors control electric lighting
- exterior solar shading, interior lightshelves, an expansive atrium skylight, and strategically placed windows to reduce the need for artificial lighting
- 28 rooftop solar panels for preheating water
- reclaimed water from neighboring zebrafish facility for flushing toilets and urinals
- operable windows with a built-in occupant notification system: red and green lights notify users when opening windows is appropriate
- a heat recovery unit to recover heat from exhaust air for reuse
- chilled beams and radiators, along with demand-control ventilation
- bamboo, a rapidly renewable building material, is the predominant wood finish material.

The Robert and Beverly Lewis Integrative Science Building is the first LEED-certified Platinum building on campus and one of the most sustainable science buildings in North America according to the architects in charge of the design of this building.

6 – Extensive use of glass along spaces adjacent to the atrium allows for transparency and connectivity inside the LISB (Photo courtesy of HDR/THA Architecture; © 2013 Lara Swimmer)

7 – Baffles atop the atrium (Photo courtesy of HDR/THA Architecture; © 2013 Lara Swimmer)

8 – Detail of the baffles atop the atrium (Photo courtesy of HDR/THA Architecture; © 2013 Lara Swimmer)

Changi Airport Terminal 3

Singapore

Year: 2007 **Architect:** Skidmore, Owings & Merrill
Client: Singapore Airlines **MEP Engineer & Daylighting
Consultant:** Durlum GmbH, Schopfheim, Germany
& Bartenbach GmbH, Aldrans / Innsbruck **Primary
Daylighting Strategy:** Roof skylights, "butterfly" daylight
diffusers, and aluminized parabolic light reflectors

Awarded the Singapore Green Mark Gold designation in 2009, Terminal 3 is the newest terminal at Singapore Changi International Airport 2. As one of the largest international airports, Terminal 3 utilizes natural light by the skylights integrated into the architectural roof design 1, 3, 7. An integral lighting solution combining daylight and artificial light favors daylight and uses electric lighting only when necessary. Thus it contributes to considerable savings in energy cost while providing a healthier day-lighting environment. Terminal 3 was specially developed for Singapore Airlines and its partners in the Star Alliance. Due to the increased size of the airport with a total of three terminals, it achieved a stronger position as a hub for the South East Asian countries in competition with Hong Kong, Kuala Lumpur, and Bangkok.

Terminal 3 houses the world's first butterfly garden in an airport. It is a tropical butterfly habitat that is home to over 1,000 butterflies and is complete with flowering plants, lush greenery, and a 20-foot grotto waterfall. Its 200 carnivorous plants cover as much floor space as 50 soccer fields.

1 - Interior of Changi Airport
Terminal 3, Singapore (Photo
courtesy: Bartenbach GmbH, Peter
Bartenbach)

2 - Changi Airport Terminal 3
(Photo courtesy: Durlum)

2

5

3 – Changi Airport Terminal 3 (Photo courtesy: Durlum)

4 – Hinged panels on top of the roof of Terminal 3 in open position (Photo courtesy: Skidmore, Owings & Merrill, Chicago)

5 – Hinged panels, or "butterflies," in nearly closed position on the roof of Terminal 3 (Photo courtesy: Bartenbach GmbH, ©Durlum)

6 – Light deflecting screens placed underneath the skylight openings inside the building (Photo courtesy: Skidmore, Owings & Merrill, Chicago)

7 – Interior of Terminal 3 (Photo courtesy: Durlum)

6

Building
Performance

In addition to 52,000m² of glass facades Terminal 3 has 919 skylights measuring 5m x 3m, with fully automatic photometric characteristics located on the 66,000m² expanse of roof 4. These skylights assure optimum natural light in the departure hall and eliminate the need for artificial lighting during most of the day. The development of these skylights fully integrated into the architecture presented a number of challenges, including sun protection and adequate daylight levels for people and interior plants.

The parabolic aluminium reflectors of the skylights allow good control of the daylight and distribute it with minimal light loss and minimal glare into the interior of the departure hall. Hinged panels hang above the skylights 4, 5. The so-called "butterflies" 5 are made of perforated anodized aluminium to allow an optimum daylight translucency. These devices are the first of their kind in the world and were major design, construction, and logistical challenges for all of the companies involved. The perforated hinged panels prevent unwanted solar gain by preventing exposure to direct sunlight. They are adjusted automatically to optimize daylighting depending on the position of the sun, the prevailing weather conditions, and available daylight. A number of sensors were installed on the roof that send relevant information to a centralized computer system which controls the panels for the entire terminal. The required daylight factor of approximately 5% is ensured when the panels are closed due the perforations within the panels. Steel frames assembled below the skylights (5m x 3m) form the substructure for the parabolic panels which reflect the light as needed.

Even when the sun is at the zenith directly above and the skylights and the panels are fully closed, the harvesting of natural light inside the building is assured due to a 20% perforation of the panels. Thus a precisely controlled amount of sunlight is utilized for illuminating the interior spaces and the building is daylit regardless of whether or not there is sunshine.

Due to realized energy savings for electric lighting, it is estimated that 2,400 tons per annum of CO_2 emissions are avoided. Due to the optimized daylight solution, the solar heat gain is kept to a minimum. The reduction in cooling loads achieved, due to the daylighting system, amounts to approximately 15,000,000 kWh/year. From an economic perspective, the daylight system is believed to redeem itself within five years.

7

Extension of the High Museum of Art

Atlanta, Georgia, USA

Year: 2005 **Architect:** Renzo Piano Building Workshop with Lord Aeck Sargent, Inc. **Client:** Municipality of Atlanta, Georgia, USA **MEP Engineer & Daylighting Consultant:** Ove Arup & Partners International, Uzun & Case Engineers **Primary Daylighting Strategy:** Light scoops, skylights

1 – Diffuse daylight inside a gallery of the Wieland Pavilion of the High Museum of Art in Atlanta, Georgia, USA (Photo courtesy: Renzo Piano RPBW)

2 – Aerial view (Photo courtesy: © Jonathan Hillyer)

The High Museum of Art, founded in 1905 as the Atlanta Art Association, is the leading art museum in the southeastern United States. Following a decade of unprecedented growth in exhibitions, community programming, and collection building, the High Museum of Art completed a major expansion designed by Renzo Piano in 2005. The project is the cornerstone of the overall upgrade of Atlanta's Woodruff Arts Center.

Three new buildings 2 provide new exhibition space as well as enhanced education and programming facilities that more than double the size of the original museum designed by Richard Meier. The new extension has a total of 16,722m² comprising 9,300m² of gallery space, 1,860m² of education space, and the rest for restaurants, retail, and other amenities.

The Wieland Pavilion 3, the largest of the three buildings, houses part of the High's permanent collection and special exhibitions. The pavilion includes a spacious lobby, coffee bar, retail shops, and visitor amenities. Enclosed bridges link the "old" High to the lobby and skyway of the new extension. A second building, the Anne Cox Chambers Wing, houses special collections and contains a glass-enclosed lobby and galleries spread over two floors. A third building, the Administrative Center, provides office space for staff. The three buildings surround an outdoor piazza.

The new extension is clad in aluminium panels painted white to conform to Richard Meier's original design.

2

3

4

5

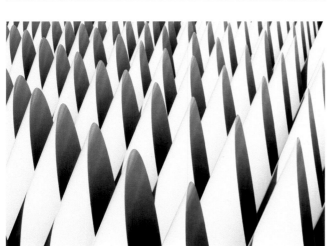

6

3 – Exterior view of the Wieland Pavilion (Photo courtesy: ARUP)

4 – Scale model testing of the light scoops (velas) (Photo courtesy: Arup)

5 – Scale model experimentation with the velas (Photo courtesy: Arup)

6 – Arrangements of the velas on top of the roof of the pavilion (Photo courtesy: Renzo Piano RPBW)

7 – View of the velas on top of the roof of the pavilion (Photo courtesy: Renzo Piano RPBW)

Building Performance

In the original building of the High Museum, the Memorial Art Building, there was little daylight. The first extension of the High, designed by Richard Meier, brought ample daylight into the museum, and sometimes too much of it. Light levels up to 10,000 lux were measured in some galleries according to the director of architectural planning and design for the High Museum (Architectural Lighting.com, 2007). These levels are much too excessive compared to the IES recommendation of 50 lux for sensitive artwork and 200 lux for less sensitive artwork.

With the new extension, corrective measures were taken to reduce exposure to UV radiation by installing UV filtering films on existing windows, and careful consideration was given to keep the daylight levels to no more than the recommended levels for artwork. According to ARUP, the lighting consultant for this project, the objectives of the new design were as follows:

– use of toplighting
– diffuse daylight throughout the gallery space
– no direct sunlight in the galleries
– UV-filtered
– passive control of daylight.

A passive daylighting approach was favored over motorized automated active systems to reduce maintenance and variability in daylight levels inside the galleries. According to the design team, an active system would have required a higher maintenance and more variability in light levels inside the galleries. Numerous scale models and real-size mock-ups as well as computer simulations were conducted to arrive at such shapes [4, 5]. The design team settled on light scoops in the shape of sails (velas in Italian). There are 1,000 velas that became the main architectural feature of the new extension both inside and outside. Arranged in 1.2m by 1m grid, the velas capture the northern diffuse light and deflect it inside to the Anne Cox Chambers Wing and Wieland Pavilion [1, 6-8].

8

The daylighting system consisted of three layers 9-11. The first layer is the north facing velas which were specially formed to allow only reflected sunlight and diffuse light inside the galleries. The second layer is comprised of the round skylights cut at an angle, with the lowest point of the slope facing north. Low iron insulated glass with PVB lamination was used to improve color temperature of the northern light and filter UVB radiation to values less than 10 microW/lumen. The third and last layer consists of 1.5m deep tubular units made of glass fiber reinforced plaster painted white. The net total transmittance of the skylight system, measured under an overcast sky between a point above the velas and the bottom of the skylight, averages 2.5%, producing an average daylight factor of 0.5% on the walls of the galleries, measured at five feet above the floor.

9

10

8 - Diffuse daylight inside a gallery of the Wieland Pavilion (Photo courtesy: Renzo Piano RPBW)

9 - Detailed view of the velas used (Photo courtesy: Renzo Piano RPBW)

10 - Section detail of a gallery with a top daylighting strategy using velas

11 - Installation of the velas (Photo courtesy: Renzo Piano RPBW)

11

CASE STUDIES

Extension of the Art Institute of Chicago

Chicago, Illinois, USA

Year: 2009 **Architect:** Renzo Piano Building Workshop and Interactive Design Inc. **Client:** City of Chicago
MEP Engineers & Daylighting Consultant: Ove Arup & Partners; Sebesta Blomberg; Carter Burgess **Primary Daylighting Strategy:** Translucent envelope

The new 24,526m^2 (264,000ft^2) wing of the Art Institute of Chicago is the largest expansion in the museum's 130-year history. The addition completes the museum campus 3. This addition designed by Renzo Piano resembles the pioneering modernist work of Mies van der Rohe. The newly added space is a lofty glass and steel structure with exposed slender steel columns. The entire structure is covered with a translucent roof called the "flying carpet" which has become a main feature of the design 1, 2, 4-9. On the first floor, the daylit court is surrounded by new educational facilities, public amenities, galleries, and a garden, linking the museum to the urban life of Chicago. The second and third floors are galleries. The third floor is completely lit by natural light through the walls and translucent roof.

1 – Entrance hall of the east wing of the Art Institute of Chicago, USA (Photo courtesy: Renzo Piano, RPBW)
2 – North facade at night (Photo courtesy: Renzo Piano, RPBW)

2

3

CASE STUDIES

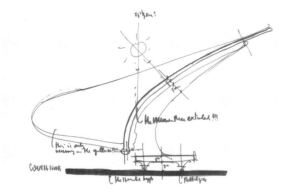

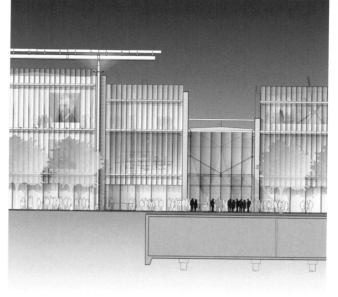

3 – Aerial view (Photo courtesy: Renzo Piano, RPBW)

4 – Conceptual sketch of the design concept of the extension (Courtesy: Renzo Piano, RPBW)

5 – Conceptual sketch of the daylighting system used in the building extension (Courtesy: Renzo Piano, RPBW)

6 – North facade: section of the east wing (Courtesy: Renzo Piano, RPBW)

7 – North facade of the extension (Courtesy: Renzo Piano, RPBW)

8 – Exterior view (Photo: M. Boubekri)

9 – The roof structure ("flying carpet") of the east wing (Photo courtesy: Renzo Piano, RPBW)

10 – Double skin facade (Photo courtesy: Renzo Piano, RPBW)

11 – The installation of the "flying carpet" (Photo courtesy: Renzo Piano, RPBW)

12 – "Flying carpet" roof structure of the east wing (Photo: M. Boubekri)

13 – Entrance hall showing the "flying carpet" translucent rook and the double skin walls (Photo courtesy: Renzo Piano, RPBW)

Building
Performance

The new addition, rectilinear and simple in form, is coiffed by a 216-foot-wide "flying carpet" canopy (as labeled by the architect) that overhangs the edge of the expansion volume. The "flying carpet" covers the glazed roof of the Modern Wing's east building to filter light and eliminate the threat of sunlight to the art. This sunshield, supported by steel bracings above the museum's third-floor galleries, is composed of thousands of extruded aluminium "blades" precisely angled to collect and redirect natural light from the north and filter out the unwanted sunlight from the south [11, 12]. "This is made easier in a city that is built on precise north-south and east-west axes, perfectly in tune with the cycle of the sun, like a solar machine," Piano wrote in notes on his original Modern Wing drawings.

Below the glass-covered ceiling are computer controlled screen and lighting controls that adjust the electrical lighting to achieve the desired lighting condition needed for viewing artwork. The daylighting design of the roof system is complemented by the Modern Wing's 76 cm thick double-skin facade of glass walls [10, 13], which help regulate and meet temperature and humidity conditions required for art while surpassing Chicago Energy Code requirements. These measures are in addition to state-of-the-art cooling and monitoring systems. The building has achieved LEED Silver certification.

11

12

13

Sino-Italian Ecological and Energy Efficient Building

Tsinghua University, Beijing, China

Year: 2006 **Architect:** Mario Cucinella Architects Srl. & Politecnico di Milano **Project leader:** Politecnico di Milano **Client:** Italian Ministry for the Environment and Land Protection, Ministry of Science and Technology of the Republic of China **Engineering and project management:** Favero & Milan Ingegneria: S. Favero, F. Zaggia, G. Lenarduzzi, L. Nicolini, China Architecture Design & Research Group **Primary Daylighting Strategy:** Louvers, lightshelves

The Sino-Italian Ecological and Energy Efficient Building (SIEEEB) 2 is a collaborative project between two governmental agencies from Italy and China. The design of this building has also been a collaborative process between architects, consultants, and researchers from both countries. Located on the Tsinghua University Campus, the building houses a Sino-Italian education, training, and research centre for environmental protection and energy conservation, offices and a 200-seat auditorium. The building has 20,000m² of floor area and is 40m high 5. The design of the building includes sustainable design features and state-of-the-art technologies that are unique to its context. The building takes its most unique look from the south side which is more transparent and comprises a series of green gardens and terraces with cantilevered structural elements containing photovoltaic panels harvest and control sunlight. The photovoltaic system placed on the south facade as well as east and west sides 6 consists of 190 modules producing a total nominal kilowatt peak power (Kwp) of 19.95. On the east and west side double-skin facades are protected by angled mirror glass panes, interior and exterior lightshelves control sunlight admission 3, 4, 6, 7. Some of the main design features of the design include a protective shell on the north side consisting of a closed highly insulated northern facade to shield the building from the cold winds during winters. Numerous computer simulations were undertaken to assess the impact of its shape and its envelope on its overall environmental performance.

2

1 - Western facade of the Sino-Italian Ecological and Energy Efficient Building in Beijing, China (Courtesy: Mario Cucinella Architects, © Daniele Domenicali).
2 - Southern terraced facade (Photo courtesy: Mario Cucinella Architects)

Building Performance

Some of the primary goals in the design of SIEEEB were energy efficiency, low CO_2 production, healthy indoor air, and minimization of environmental impact. Over 1,000m² of photovoltaic panels supply primary energy needs. Particular attention has been given to the enhancement of natural light through the study of a lightshelf integrated in the facade. Electric lighting is controlled both electronically and manually. Photosensors placed in the offices and laboratories control the ballast of the fluorescent lighting system used therein. A manual lighting dimming system is also located in these spaces where users can adjust their lighting according to their lighting preferences. According to simulation models performed at the Institute in Milan, Italy, SIEEEB will be saving approximately 1,000 tons of CO_2 emissions per year, a 58% reduction compared to conventional buildings and has the potential for an 80% reduction if the building is able to produce excess energy sold back to the national grid according to a study conducted by the University Design Consortium (UDC, 2013) at Arizona State University.

3 – Detail section of the double skin facade and exterior/internal lightshelves on the east and west walls (Courtesy: Mario Cucinella Architects)

4 – Close-up view showing the double-skin facade and exterior/internal lightshelves on the west wall (Photo courtesy: Mario Cucinella Architects)

5 – Section showing building heights and spatial organization (Courtesy: Mario Cucinella Architects)

6 – Photovoltaic panels with terraced gardens on the south facade and reflective louvers on the south and east walls (Photo courtesy: Mario Cucinella Architects)

7 – Reflective louvers on the west wall (Photo courtesy: Mario Cucinella Architects)

3

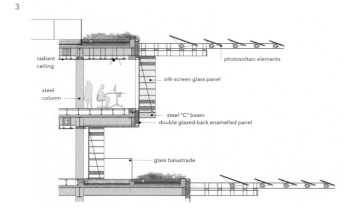

radiant ceiling

steel column

photovoltaic elements

silk-screen glass panel

steel "C" beam
double glazed back enamelled panel

glass balustrade

4

5

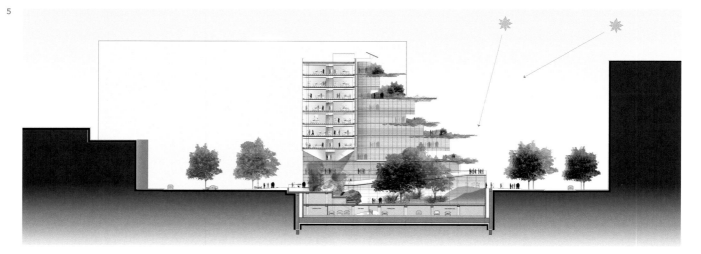

8

8 – Interior view of the library (Courtesy: Mario Cucinella Architects, © Daniele Domenicali)

9 – Tall windows and high mounted clerestory admit daylight deep inside the SIEEEB (Courtesy: Mario Cucinella Architects, © Daniele Domenicali)

10 – Reflective pool inside a courtyard (Courtesy: Mario Cucinella Architects, © Daniele Domenicali)

9

Cathedral of Christ the Light

Oakland, California, USA

Year: 2008 **Architect:** Skidmore, Owings & Merrill LLP, Craig Hartman, FAIA, Design Partner **Client:** Catholic Diocese of Oakland **MEP Engineer / Daylighting Consultant:** The Engineering Enterprise, Korve Engineering, Taylor Engineering, Claude R. Engle, Lighting, Shen Milsom & Wilke, Inc. **Primary Daylighting Strategy:** Double skin translucent envelope and louver system

1 - Interior view of the Cathedral of Christ the Light, Oakland, USA (Photo courtesy: Skidmore, Owings & Merrill; © Skidmore, Owings & Merrill LLP 2013, © Cesar Rubio)

2 - Exterior view (Photo courtesy: Skidmore, Owings & Merrill; © Skidmore, Owings & Merrill LLP 2013, © Cesar Rubio)

The Cathedral of Christ the Light, a 226,000ft² (21,000m²) complex sits on 2.5-acre site and is the home to the Oakland Diocese 2, 3. Designed by Skidmore, Owings & Merrill, the sanctuary – the central feature of the complex – sits on a poured-in-place concrete podium that houses a mix of uses, including a legal clinic, a health clinic, a conference center, and administration offices for the diocese 6. An interior courtyard carved within the podium dotted with skylights provides generous daylight to the underground spaces.

The diocese, the client, challenged the design team to create a building that is architecturally unique, that will last a long time, and that can be remembered. The design team, led by architect Craig Hartman, FAIA, embraced a non-rectilinear approach to the design. The sanctuary, 118 feet high and seating 1,350 people with curvilinear forms, fuses harmoniously a cone-shaped glass outer shell and a spherical ribbed louvered inner layer made of Douglas fir wood 1, 4, 5, 7. This wooden layer boasts a total of 724 narrowly spaced louver elements that intersect and provide lateral bracing and structural support for inner rib members. The two forms unite at the base and repose on an oval poured-in-site-concrete pedestal made of fly ash and slag, a residual byproduct of coal combustion and steel production which reduces the use of cement. The concrete pedestal also serves as thermal mass and heat sink for passive solar heating.

2

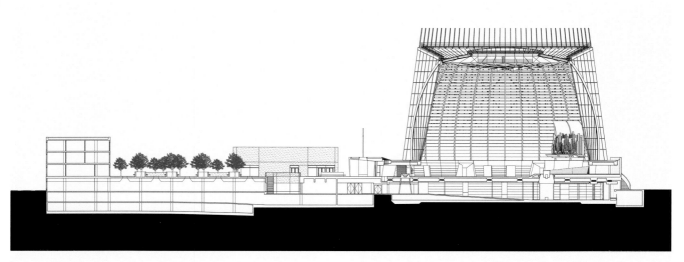

0   32   64

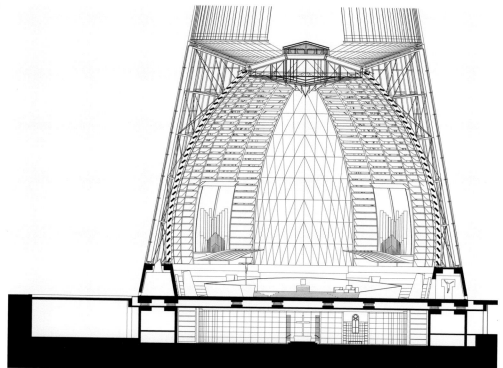

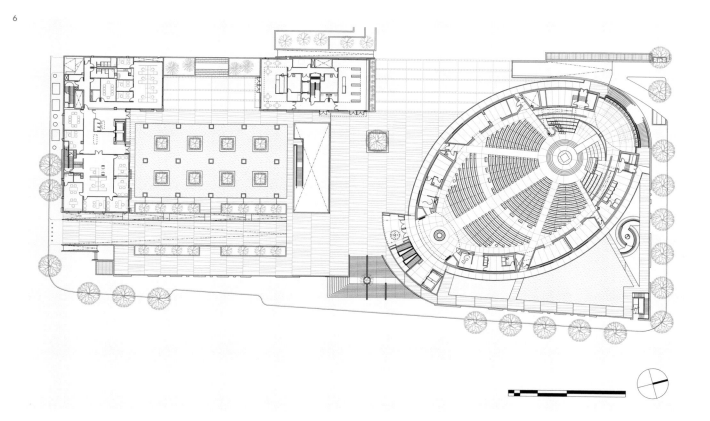

Building Performance

The daylighting design of the sanctuary has practical as well as symbolic implications. On a symbolic level and as its name suggests, the Cathedral of Christ the Light draws on the tradition of the concept of light as a sacred phenomenon. On a practical level, the transparent outer layer combines laminated glass and clear low-e glass that provides high luminous quality inside the sanctuary while avoiding glare. Indirect daylight filters through the louvered Douglas-fir fins and the almond-shaped oculus atop the structure into the sanctuary 9. In sunny conditions, the scrim-like exterior glass layer of the sanctuary admits diffuse light which is filtered again by the louvered wooden inner layer of the sanctuary. The veil fabric below the oculus of the skylight provides an interesting geometric pattern of contrasting sunlight and shadows sparkling on the floors and walls of the sanctuary, enlivening the space with additional vibrancy and excitement 8. The omnidirectional character of light inside the sanctuary imitates the universal character of daylight outside but with less intensity, eliminating henceforth any risks of discomfort, direct or reflected glare inside the sanctuary.

This project received more than 30 national and international awards, including the American Institute of Architects (AIA) National Honor Award for Interior Architecture, AIA National Honor Award for Architecture, AIA San Francisco Chapter Excellence in Architecture Honor Award.

7 – Detail of the double skin construction (Photo courtesy: Skidmore, Owings & Merrill; © Skidmore, Owings & Merrill LLP 2013)

8 – Sunlight pattern inside the cathedral (Photo courtesy: Skidmore, Owings & Merrill; © Skidmore, Owings & Merrill LLP 2013, © Cesar Rubio)

9 – The oculus atop the Christ figure (Photo courtesy: Skidmore, Owings & Merrill; © Skidmore, Owings & Merrill LLP 2013, © Cesar Rubio)

7

8

1

Schlaues Haus

Oldenburg, Germany

Year: 2012 **Architect:** Behnisch Architekten
Client: Schlaues Haus Oldenburg gGmbH **MEP**
Engineer: Ingenieurbüro Ahrens GmbH **Climate**
Engineer: Transsolar Energietechnik GmbH
Contractor Facade: Oltmanns Metallbau GmbH
Daylighting Consultants: Transsolar Energie-
technik GmbH **Primary Daylighting Strategy:**
Skylights, light wells, intelligent facade

1 – Interior of the Schlaues
Haus showing the light well and
skylights on the roof, Oldenburg,
Germany (Photographer: Meike
Hansen)

2 – View of the main entrance
and the south facade of the
Schlaues Haus (Photographer:
Meike Hansen)

3 – Revitalization on the
narrow site in the inner-city area
(© Behnisch Architekten)

2

The Schlaues Haus Oldenburg ("Smart House") is first and foremost a public building, in which regional scientific knowledge and accomplishments are exhibited. The centrally located building 3 is an important point of reference for visitors to Oldenburg due to placement of the city tourist information center on the ground floor of the building. Here, citizens and visitors alike are informed about scientific topics such as energy and climate protection and life and living in the future.

The sustainability concept of the building begins with the choice of the site. The Schlaues Haus is located in the Schlossplatz (Castle Square) directly in the center of Oldenburg. Situated in a historic quarter with a development structure that has grown organically, it links the Oldenburger Castle in the north with the adjacent castle gardens to the south of the site. The oldest building of the city, an abandoned community center from the 16th century, was renovated and extended in the rear section.

The idea of a "smart" or "intelligent" building is also reflected in the architectural concept of the design. It is energy-efficient, sustainable, and flexible in its use. The building style of the neighboring building, with its various floors, is integrated on both sides – both on the levels themselves and in the facades. Within the Schlaues Haus, the transition between the existing building and the new building can be experienced directly via the staggered, split levels 5, 6. The adaption of the existing building to its new use and of the necessary addition is visible as a result of an intentional juxtaposition of the different building styles and structure of the space. Larger ceiling heights and open floor plans throughout a range of levels create a sense of lightness despite the massive, solid building components, and serve to characterize the new building, which visitors access via the narrower, historic building.

3

5

4 – Different inclinations of the individual areas of the south facade minimize the heat entry during the summer months (Photographer: Meike Hansen)

5 & 6 – The dialogue between old and new is emphasized by a building-high interstice, accentuating the split levels of both building sections (Photographer: Meike Hansen)

7 – Interior of the Schlaues Haus showing the light well and skylights in the roof (Photographer: Meike Hansen)

8 & 9 – Daylight and natural ventilation concepts (© Behnisch Architekten)

10 – User-based annual primary energy use (© Transsolar)

6

Building Performance

The goal of the planning team was to develop a building that minimizes the demand for energy using passive measures, reducing the use by means of efficient technologies, and meeting any remaining energy demands through the use of local energy sources such as photovoltaic.

The themes of daylight and the goal of creating a passive, intelligent building defined the design concept 8, 9. The passive, sustainable measures include, in addition to a daylight corridor for a light-flooded building, the new south facade that is also oriented towards the Schlosspark (Castle Gardens). At the same time, the daylight corridor has the appearance of a solar draught tube and, in this way, enhances the natural ventilation. Particular attention was paid to the design of the new south-facing glass facade. Through the inclination of the individual sections, the heat input during the summer months is minimized 4 and the south facade is given its distinct character by an innovative sun-shading device, a foil with micro-lamellae, integrated into the interspace between the sheets of glass. The building shell, developed in simulations to optimize the daylight entry, ensures an excellent balance between solar energy gain in summer and minimum heat loss in winter.

The vertical and horizontal skylights ensure the supply of daylight inside the building 1, 7 and provide views to the outside. A combination of sun protection on the interior, natural rear ventilation, and a low level of infrared emissivity in the interior allows for the use of selected quality sunscreening and triplex glass. The design of the building with regard to the daylight entry has been optimized to respond to a diffuse, overcast sky. The sunshading facility effectively prevents overheating in summer as well as high gradients of light intensity.

The following energy target values were set for the building:
- solar construction 100 kWh/m² a primary energy requirements
- zero energy balance for the building operations via integrated PV surfaces.

The overall annual energy consumption of the building with reference to an area of 900m² was calculated during the design phase taking into account extreme conditions. The calculated annual electricity requirement for the building operations is 27.1 kWh/m²a. With regard to a reference area of 900m² this generates 24.4 MWh/a. This value is equivalent to approximately 28 x 100W bulbs in continuous operation for the whole building (a 100W bulb in continuous operation = approximately 1 kWh/m²a). The primary energy requirements for the building operations is 73 kWh/m²a, while the user-specific requirements (projector, PC) are 43 kWh/m²a.

The concept of flexibility is reflected in the use of different facade elements. For example, blinds/louvers which can be easily controlled, were utilized, granting users to the ability to adapt them individually to their needs – a factor that is critical with regards to the acceptance of such a system. The use of robust systems should also be emphasized. Secure systems that do not require maintenance avoid the danger of operating errors and do not require active controlling as the g-value changes ultimately with the position of the sun.

8

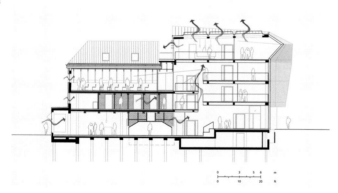

9

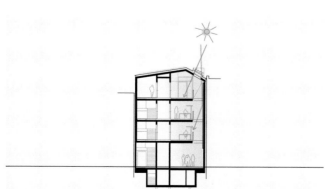

10

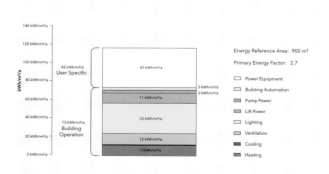

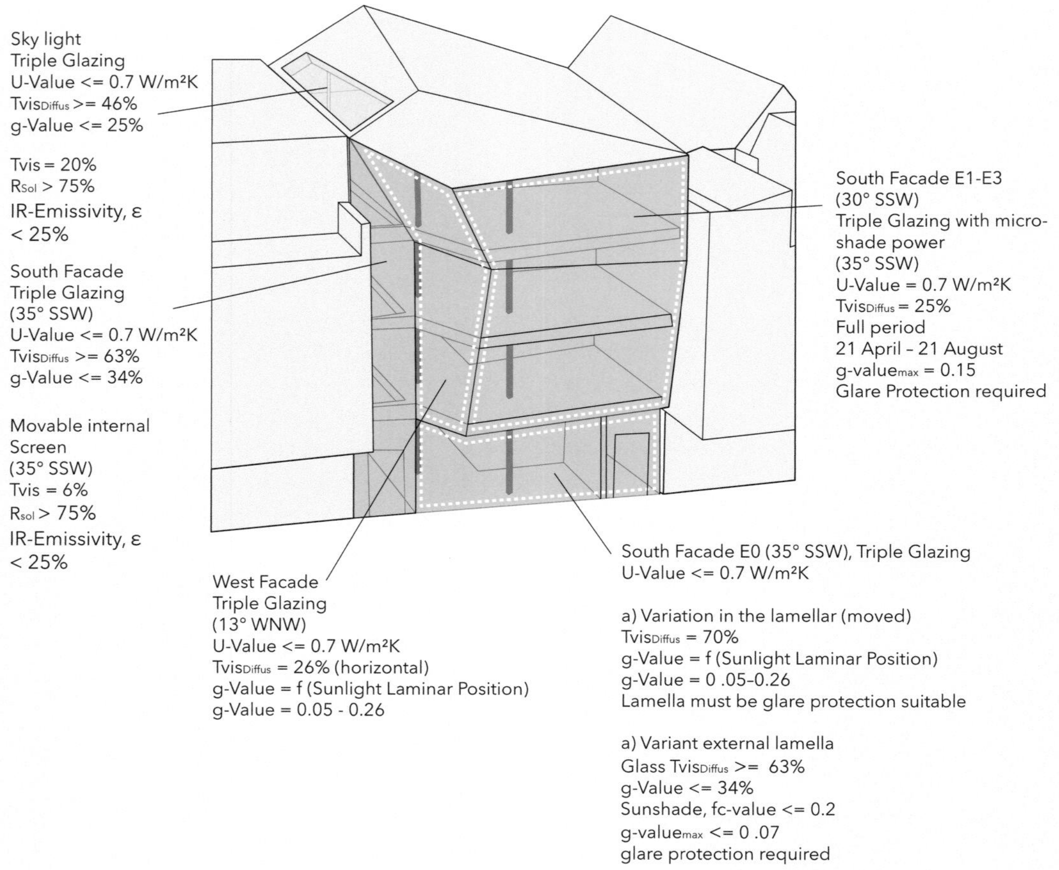

Sky light
Triple Glazing
U-Value <= 0.7 W/m²K
$Tvis_{Diffus}$ >= 46%
g-Value <= 25%

Tvis = 20%
R_{sol} > 75%
IR-Emissivity, ε
< 25%

South Facade
Triple Glazing
(35° SSW)
U-Value <= 0.7 W/m²K
$Tvis_{Diffus}$ >= 63%
g-Value <= 34%

Movable internal
Screen
(35° SSW)
Tvis = 6%
R_{sol} > 75%
IR-Emissivity, ε
< 25%

South Facade E1-E3
(30° SSW)
Triple Glazing with micro-
shade power
(35° SSW)
U-Value = 0.7 W/m²K
$Tvis_{Diffus}$ = 25%
Full period
21 April – 21 August
g-value$_{max}$ = 0.15
Glare Protection required

West Facade
Triple Glazing
(13° WNW)
U-Value <= 0.7 W/m²K
$Tvis_{Diffus}$ = 26% (horizontal)
g-Value = f (Sunlight Laminar Position)
g-Value = 0.05 - 0.26

South Facade E0 (35° SSW), Triple Glazing
U-Value <= 0.7 W/m²K

a) Variation in the lamellar (moved)
$Tvis_{Diffus}$ = 70%
g-Value = f (Sunlight Laminar Position)
g-Value = 0 .05–0.26
Lamella must be glare protection suitable

a) Variant external lamella
Glass $Tvis_{Diffus}$ >= 63%
g-Value <= 34%
Sunshade, fc-value <= 0.2
g-value$_{max}$ <= 0 .07
glare protection required

11 – Features and use of micro-lamella glazing and PV glazing in the south facade (© Transsolar)

12 – Use of micro-lamella glazing and PV glazing in the south facade (Photographer: Meike Hansen)

13 – Properties of micro-louver windows and the PV glazing within the south facade (© Behnisch Architekten)

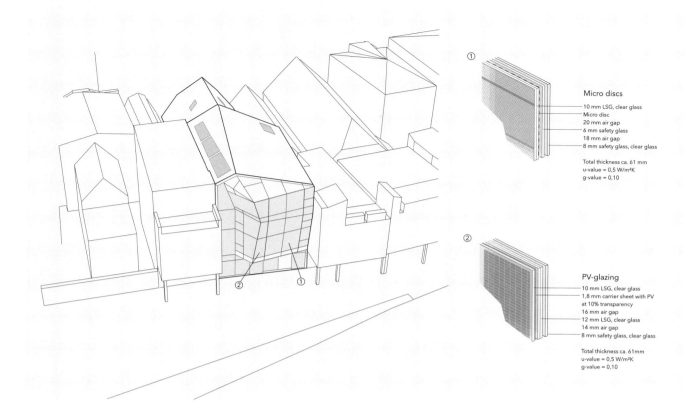

① Micro discs

10 mm LSG, clear glass
Micro disc
20 mm air gap
6 mm safety glass
18 mm air gap
8 mm safety glass, clear glass

Total thickness ca. 61 mm
u-value = 0,5 W/m²K
g-value = 0,10

② PV-glazing

10 mm LSG, clear glass
1,8 mm carrier sheet with PV
at 10% transparency
16 mm air gap
12 mm LSG, clear glass
14 mm air gap
8 mm safety glass, clear glass

Total thickness ca. 61mm
u-value = 0,5 W/m²K
g-value = 0,10

Bibliography

Acheson, E. D., C. A. Bachrach, and F.M. Wright. 1960. "Some Comments on the Relationship of the Distribution of Multiple Sclerosis to Latitude, Solar Radiation and Other Variables." *Acta Psychiatrica Neurologica Scandinavica Supplementum* 147: 132–147.

Aizenburg, J. B. 1997. "Principal New Hollow Light Guide System 'Heliobus' for Daylighting and Artificial Lighting of Central Zones of Multi Storey Buildings." *Right Light* 4(2): 239–243.

Aizlewood, M. 2001. "Assessment of Glare." *Monitoring Procedures for the Assessment of Daylighting. Performance of Buildings. A Report of the IEA SHC Task 21*, edited by M. Veld and J. Christoffersen, Brussels, ECBS Annex 29.

Akerstedt, T., C. A. Czeisler, D. F. Dinges, and J. A. Horne. 1994. "Accidents and Sleepiness–A Consensus Statement." *Journal of Sleep Research* 3(4): 195.

Al-Badr, W., and K. J. Martin. 2008. "Vitamin D and Kidney Disease." *Clinical Journal of the American Society of Nephrology* 3: 1555–1560.

Altherr, R., and J-B. Gay. 2002. "A Low Environmental Impact Anidolic Facade." *Building and Environment* 37(12): 1409–1419.

American Institute of Architects. 2013. iatopten.org/node/265 (retrieved November 25, 2013).

Ando, T. 1991. "From the Periphery of Architecture." *Japan Architect* 1(1): 19.

Anninos, W. Y., and M. Boubekri. 1996. "Daylight Distribution in Atrium Spaces with the Glazing as a Lambertian Light Source; Part 3: The Linear-Open-End Atrium." *Architectural Science Review* 39(4): 179–186.

ArchitecturalLighting.com. 2007. "Measuring Daylight at High Museum," posted March 8, 2007.

Aries, M. B. C., S. H. A. Begemann, A. D. Tenner, and L. Zonnevedt. 2003. "Retinal Illuminance: A New Design Parameter?" Proceedings of the 25th Session of the CIE, San Diego, CA.

Arnesen, H. 2003. "Performance of Daylighting Systems for Sidelighted Spaces at High Latitudes." PhD diss., Norwegian University of Science and Technology, Faculty of Architecture and Fine Art.

Arney, E., J. Spiker, H. Schepers, and A. Rosenthal. n.d. "Let There Be Light." Woodsbagot.com. www.woodsbagot.com/en/Documents/Let_There_Be_Light.pdf (retrieved October 30, 2012).

Association Suisse des Electriciens. 1989. "Eclairage intérieur par la lumière du jour." Association Suisse des Electriciens, Swiss Norm SN 418911, Zurich.

Avery, D. H., and M. J. Norden. 1998. "Dawn Simulation and Bright Light Therapy in Subsyndromal Seasonal Affective Disorder." *Seasonal Affective Disorder and Beyond: Light Treatment for SAD and Non-SAD Conditions*, edited by R. W. Lam. Washington, DC: American Psychiatric Press, 143–158.

Beauchemin, K. M., and P. Hays. 1996. "Sunny Hospital Rooms Expedite Recovery from Severe and Refractory Depressions." *Journal of Affective Disorders* 40: 49–51.

Beauchemin, K. M., and P. Hays. 1998. "Dying in the Dark: Sunshine, Gender and Outcomes in Myocardial Infarction." *Journal of the Royal Society of Medicine* 91: 352–354.

Belcher, C. M., and R. Kluczny. 1987. "Lighting Ergonomics and the Decision Process." Proceedings from the annual meeting of the American Society for Engineering Management, 51–54.

Benedetti, F., C. Colombo, B. Barbini, et al. 2001. "Morning Sunlight Reduces Length of Hospitalization in Bipolar Depression." *Journal of Affective Disorders* 62(3): 221–223.

Bennett, D., and D. Eijad. 1980. "Solar Optics: Projecting Light into Buildings." *AIA Journal* 69: 72–74.

Berger, A. M., B. R. Kuhn, L. A. Farr, et al. 2009. "Behavioral Therapy Intervention Trial to Improve Sleep Quality and Cancer-Related Fatigue." *Psycho-Oncology* 18(6): 634–646.

Boubekri, M. 1992a. "Performance of a Light-Shelf Considering its Height and Depth at High Northern Latitude." Proceedings of North Sun '92 Solar Energy at High Latitudes Conference, Trondheim, Norway, June.

Boubekri, M. 1992b. "Impact of Position on the Performance of a Light Shelf." Proceedings of American Solar Energy Conference, Cocoa-Beach, FL, June 13–18.

Boubekri, M. 1995. "Appraisal of the Lighting Condition in an Office Building: Results of a Survey." *Indoor Environment* 4: 162–169.

Boubekri, M. 1999. "An Experimental Evaluation of the Efficiency of Prismatic Glazing Systems." Proceedings of the 16th International Conference on Passive and Low Energy Architecture, Brisbane, Australia, September 18–26.

Boubekri, M. 2000. "On the Issues of Illuminance Requirements as a Design Criterion." *Journal of the Human-Environment System* 3(1): 71–76.

Boubekri, M. 2008. *Daylighting, Architecture, and Health: Design Strategies*. Oxford: Architectural Press.

Boubekri, M., R. B. Hull IV, and L. L. Boyer. 1991. "Impact of Window Size and Sunlight Penetration on Office Workers' Mood and Satisfaction: A Novel Way of Assessing Sunlight." *Environment and Behavior* 23(4): 474–493.

Boubekri, M., and L. L. Boyer. 1992. "Effect of Window Size and Sunlight Presence on Glare." *Lighting Research and Technology* 24(2): 69–74.

Boubekri, M., and W. Y. Anninos. 1995. "Skylight Wells: A Finite Element Approach to Analysis of Efficiency." *Lighting Research and Technology* 27(3): 153–159.

Boubekri, M., and W. Y. Anninos. 1996a. "Daylight Distribution in Atrium Spaces with the Glazing as a Lambertian Light Source; Part I: The Four-Sided Atrium." *Architectural Science Review* 39(2): 25–31.

Boubekri, M., and W. Y. Anninos. 1996b. "Daylight Distribution in Atrium Spaces with the Glazing as a Lambertian Light Source; Part 2: The Three-Sided Atrium." *Architectural Science Review* 39(2): 83–88.

Boubekri, M., and N. Wang. 2012. "A Post-Hoc Analysis of the Combined Effect of Multiple Environmental Factors in Daylighting Design." *Journal of the Human-Environment System* 14(2): 49–59.

Boubekri, M., I. Cheung, P. Zee, et al. 2014. "Impact of Windows and Daylight Exposure on Overall Health and Sleep Quality of Office Workers: A Case-Control Pilot Study," submitted for review.

Bower, B., L. M. Bylsma, B. H. Morris, and J. Rottenberg. 2010. "Reported Sleep Quality Predicts Low Positive Affect in Daily Life Among Healthy and Mood-Disordered Persons." *Journal of Sleep Research* 19: 323–332.

Boyce, P. R. 2003. *Human Factors in Lighting*. London and New York: Taylor & Francis.

Boyce, P. R., and D. J. Kennaway. 1987. "Effects of Light on Melatonin Production." *Biological Psychiatry* 22: 473–478.

Callow, J. 2003. "Daylighting Using Tubular Light Guides," PhD diss., University of Nottingham.

Carla, S., C. Möller-Levet, S. N. Archer, et al. 2013. "Effects of Insufficient Sleep on Circadian Rhythmicity and Expression Amplitude of the Human Blood Transcriptome." Proceedings of the National Academy of Sciences of the United States of America.

Carter, D. J. 2002. "The Measured and Predicted Performance of Passive Solar Light Pipe Systems." *Lighting Research and Technology* 34(1): 39–52.

Center for Energy & Climate Solutions. 2013. www.cool-companies.org (accessed November 25, 2013).

Chauvel, P., and R. Dogniaux. 1982. "Glare from Windows: Current Views of the Problem." *Lighting Research and Technology* 14(1): 31–46.

Chen, S., X-P Ni, M. H. Humphreys, and D. G. Gardner. 2005. "1,25 Dihydroxyvitamin D Amplifies Type A Natriuretic Peptide Receptor Expression and Activity in Target Cells." *Journal of the American Society of Nephrology* 16: 329–39.

Claros, S. T., and A. Soler. 2001. "Indoor Daylight Climate–Comparison Between Light Shelves and Overhand Performances in Madrid for Hours with Unit Sunshine Fraction and Realistic Values of Model Reflectance." *Solar Energy* 71(4): 233–239.

Claros, S. T., and A. Soler. 2002. "Indoor Daylight Climate-Influence of Light Shelf and Model Reflectance on Light Shelf Performance in Madrid for Hours with Unit Sunshine Fraction." *Building and Environment* 37: 587–598.

Cofaigh, E. O., E. Fitzgerald, R. Alcock, J. O., et al. 1999. *A Green Vitruvius: Principles and Practice of Sustainable Architectural Design*. London: James & James.

Coss, R. G. 1991. "Evolutionary Persistence of Memory-Like Processes." *Concepts in Neuroscience* 2: 129–168.

Courret, G. 1999. "Anidolic Daylighting Systems." PhD diss. no. 2026. Department of Architecture, EPFL, Lausanne, Switzerland.

Courret, G., J. L. Scartezzini, D. Francioli, and J. J. Meyer. 1998. "Design and Assessment of an Anidolic Light-Duct." *Energy and Buildings* 28: 79–99.

Davenport, C. B. 1922. "Multiple Sclerosis from the Standpoint of Geographic Distribution and Race." *Archives of Neurology and Psychiatry* 8: 51–58.

DeLuca, H. F. 1988. "The Vitamin D Story: A Collaborative Effort of Basic Science and Clinical Medicine." *FASEB Journal* 2: 224–236.

DIN V 18599-4. 2005. "Energy Performance of Buildings – Part 4: Lighting."

Dinges, D. F., R. C. Graeber, M. A. Carskadon, et al. 1989. "Attending to Inattention." *Science* 245(4916): 342.

Djukic, M., C. Kovner, W. C. Budin, and R. Norman. 2010. "Physical Work Environment: Testing an Expanded Model of Job Satisfaction in a Sample of Registered Nurses." *Journal of Nursing Research* 59(6): 441–451.

Dubois, M. C. 2001. "Impact of Shading Devices on Daylight Quality in Offices: Simulations with Radiance." Retrieved September, 15, 2006, from http://www.byggark.lth.se/shade/shade_home.html.

Edmonds, I. 1993. "Performance of Laser Cut Light Deflecting Panels in Daylighting Applications." *Solar Energy Materials and Solar Cells* 29: 1–26.

Edmonds, I. R., and P. J. Greenup. 2002. "Daylighting in the Tropics." *Solar Energy* 73(2): 111–121.

Elton, J. M. 1920. *A Study of Output in Silk Weaving During Winter Months*. London: His Majesty's Stationery Office.

Energy Center of Wisconsin. 2005. "Energy Savings from Daylighting," ECW Report Number 233-1.

Enermodal Engineering Ltd for Public Works & Government Services Canada. 2002. "Daylighting Guide for Canadian Commercial Buildings."

Farrenkopf, T., and V. Roth. 1980. "The University Faculty Office as an Environment. *Environment and Behavior* 12: 467–477.

Francis, M., and R. T. Hester Jr., eds. 1995. *The Meaning of Gardens*. Cambridge, MA: MIT Press.

Freewan, A. A. 2010. "Maximizing the Lightshelf Performance by Interaction Between Lightshelf Geometries and a Curved Ceiling." *Energy Conversion and Management* 51(8): 1600–1604.

Gandini, S., M. Boniol, J. Haukka, et al. 2011. "Meta-Analysis of Observational Studies of Serum 25-Hydroxyvitamin D Levels and Colorectal, Breast and Prostate Cancer and Colorectal Adenoma." *International Journal of Cancer* 128(6): 1414-1424.

Garcia-Hansen, V., and I. Edmonds. 2003. "Natural Illumination of Deep-Plan Office Buildings: Light Pipe Strategies." In ISES Solar World Congress 2003, Gothenburg, Sweden, June 14-19.

Garland, C., and F. Garland. 1980. "Do Sunlight and Vitamin D Reduce the Likelihood of Colon Cancer?" *International Journal of Epidemiology* 9: 227-231.

Gerlach-Spriggs, N., R. E. Kaufman, and S. B. Warner. 1998. *Restorative Gardens: The Healing Landscape*. New Haven: Yale University Press.

Ghannam, N. N., M. M. Hammami, S. M. Bakheet, and B. A. Khan. 1999. "Bone Mineral Density of the Spine and Femur in Healthy Saudi Females: Relation to Vitamin D Status, Pregnancy, and Lactation." *Calcified Tissue International* 65: 23-28.

Giesen, M., and C. Hendrick. 1974. "Effects of Seating Distance and Room Illumination on the Affective Outcome of Small Group Interaction." *Journal of Social Behavior & Personality* 2: 87-96.

Giovannucci, E. 1998. "Dietary Influences of 1,25(OH)2 Vitamin D in Relation to Prostate Cancer: A Hypothesis." *Cancer Causes Control* 9: 567-582.

Glerup, H., K. Mikkelsen, L. Poulsen, et al. 2001. "Commonly Recommended Daily Intake of Vitamin D is not Sufficient if Sunlight Exposure is Limited." *Journal of Internal Medicine* 247(2): 260-268.

Gorham, E. D., C. F. Garland, F. C. Garland, et al. 2005. "Vitamin D and Prevention of Colorectal Cancer." *Journal of Steroid Biochemistry & Molecular Biology* 97: 179-194.

Grant, W. B., and C. F. Garland. 2006. "The Association of Solar Ultraviolet B (UVB) with Reducing Risk of Cancer: Multifactorial Ecologic Analysis of Geographic Variation in Age-Adjusted Cancer Mortality Rates." *Anticancer Research* 26: 2687-2700.

Greenberg, P. E., Ronald C. Kessler, H. G. Birnbaum, et al. 2003. "The Economic Burden of Depression in the United States: How Did It Change Between 1990 and 2000?" *Journal of Clinical Psychiatry* 64(12): 1465-1475.

Guardian. 2006. "Depression Is UK's Biggest Social Problem, Government Told." April 27.

Hartig, T., M. Mang, and G. W. Evans. 1991. "Restorative Effects of Natural Environment Experiences." *Environment and Behavior* 23(1): 3-26.

Hawton, K. 1992. "Suicide and Attempted Suicide." *Handbook of Affective Disorders*. E. S. Paykel. New York: Guilford Press: 635-650.

Hay, A., and R. Parlane. 2011. "Okanagan College Centre of Excellence in Sustainable Building Technologies and Renewable Energy Conservation." *Journal of Green Building* 6(1): 14-24.

Hellekson, C. J. 1989. "Phenomenology of Seasonal Affective Disorder: An Alaskan Perspective." *Seasonal Affective Disorder and Phototherapy,* edited by N. E. Rosenthal. New York: Guildford Press.

Herzog, T. 2006 (September). "Extension to the Head Office of SOKA-BAU, the Pensions and Benefits Fund of the German Building Industry, in Wiesbaden: A New Multi-Use Building with Offices, Restaurant, Conference, Computer Center, 1994-2004." PLEA Conference, 608.

Herzog, T. 2006. *Soka Bau: Nutzung Effizienz Nachhaltigkeit/ Utility Sustainability Efficiency*. Munich and New York: Prestel Publishing.

Herzog, T. R., A. M. Black, K. A. Fountaine, and D. J. Knotts. 1997. "Reflection and Attentional Recovery as Distinctive Benefits of Restorative Environments." *Journal of Environmental Psychology* 17: 165-170.

Heschong Mahone Group. 1999a. "Daylighting in Schools." Pacific Gas and Electric Company on behalf of the California Board for Energy Efficiency Third Party Program. August.

Heschong Mahone Group. 1999b. "Skylight and Retail Sales: An Investigation into the Relationship Between Daylighting and Human Performance." Pacific Gas and Electric Company.

Heschong Mahone Group. 2003. "Daylight and Retail Sales." Technical Report No. P500-03-082-A-5 prepared for the California Energy Commission. October.

Hesselgren, S. 1975. *Man's Perception of Man-made Environment*. Lund, Sweden: Studentlitteratur ab.

Higgins, D. M., Kelly M. Queensland, P. E. Wischmeyer, et al. 2012. "Relationship of Vitamin D Deficiency to Clinical Outcomes in Critically Ill Patients." *Journal of Parenteral and Enteral Nutrition* 36(6): 713-720.

Hobbs, R. D., Z. Habib, D. Alromaihi, et al. 2009. "Severe Vitamin D Deficiency in Arab-American Women Living in Dearborn, Michigan." *Endocrine Practice* 15(1): 35-40.

Holick, M. F. 2004. "Vitamin D: Importance in the Prevention of Cancers, Type 1 Diabetes, Heart Disease, and Osteoporosis." *American Journal of Clinical Nutrition* 79: 362-71.

Holladay, L. L. 1926. "The Fundamentals of Glare Visibility." *Journal of the Optical Society of North America*, 12: 271-319.

Hopkinson, R. G. 1963. *Architectural Physics: Lighting*. London: HMSO.

Hopkinson, R. G., P. Petherbridge, and J. Longmore. 1966. *Daylighting*. London: Heinemann.

Hopkinson, R. G. 1972. "Glare from Daylighting, in Buildings." *Applied Ergonomics* 3(4): 206-215.

Horsburgh, C. R. 1995. "Healing by Design." *New England Journal of Medicine* 333 (11): 735-740.

Iler, R. K., S. Ballal, T. Laike, et al. 2006. "The Impact of Light and Colour on Psychological Mood: A Cross-Cultural Study of Indoor Work Environments." *Journal of Ergonomics* 49(14): 1496-1507.

Illuminating Engineering Society of North America. 2000. *Lighting Handbook*, 9th edition, edited by M. S. Rea. New York.

Inderjeeth, C. A., T. Barett, M. J. Al-Lahham, et al. 2002 (April). "Seasonal Variation, Hip Fracture and Vitamin D Levels in Southern Tasmania." *New Zealand Medical Journal* 26(1152): 183-185.

Inkarojrit, V. 2005. "Balancing Comfort: Occupants' Control of Window Blinds in Private Offices." PhD diss., Department of Architecture, University of California, Berkeley.

Inoue, T., and K. Itoh. 1989. "Methodological Study of Dynamic Evaluation of Discomfort Glare." *Journal of Architecture, Planning and Environmental Engineering, Transaction of the Architects Institute of Japan* 398: 9-19.

International Energy Agency (IEA). 2012. "World Energy Outlook 2012." http://www.iea.org/publications/freepublications/publication/English.pdf (retrieved April 2013).

IOM (Institute of Medicine). 2000. *To Err Is Human: Building a Safer Health System*. Washington, DC: National Academy Press.

Isen, A. M., B. Means, R. Patrick, and G. P. Nowicki. 1982. "Some Factors Influencing Decision-Making Strategy and Risk Taking." *Affect and Cognition*, edited by M. Clark and S. Fiske. Hillsdale, NJ: Lawrence Erlbaum Associates.

Iwata, T., and M. Tokura. 1998. "Examination of the Limitations of Predicted Glare Sensation Vote (PGSV) as a Glare Index for a Large Source." *Lighting Research & Technology* 30(2): 81-88.

Jakubiec, J. A., and C. F. Reinhart. 2012. "The 'Adaptive Zone' – A Concept for Assessing Discomfort Glare Throughout Daylit Spaces." *Lighting Research & Technology* 44: 149-170.

Joiner, T. 2010. *Myths About Suicide*. Cambridge: Harvard University Press, 288.

Keep, P., J. James, and M. Inman. 1980. "Windows in the Intensive Therapy Unit." *Anaesthesia* 35: 257-262.

Kessler, R. C., C. Barber, H. G. Birnbaum, et al. 1999. "Depression in the Workplace: Effects on Short-Term Disability." *Health Affairs* 18: 163-171.

Kim, J. T., G. Y. Yun, and J. Y. Shin. 2011. "Prediction of Discomfort Glare from Windows: Influence of the Subjective Evaluation of Window Views." Fifth International Symposium on Sustainable Healthy Buildings, Seoul, Korea, February 10.

King, A. J., and C. H. Parsons. 1999. "Improved Auditory Spatial Acuity in Visually Deprived Ferrets." *European Journal of Neuroscience* 11: 3945-3956.

Knez, I. 1995. "Effect of Indoor Lighting on Mood and Cognition." *Journal of Environmental Psychology* 15: 39-51.

Knutson, K. L., A. M. Ryden, et al. 2006. "Role of Sleep Duration and Quality in the Risk and Severity of Type 2 Diabetes Mellitus." *Archives of Internal Medicine* 166(16): 1768-1774.

Kuller, B., and C. Lindsten. 1992. "Health and Behavior of Children in Classrooms with and without windows." *Journal of Environmental Psychology* 12: 305-317.

Küller, R. 1996. "The Subterranean Work Environment: Impact on Well-Being and Health." *Environment International* 22(1): 33-52.

Laar, M. 2001. "Daylighting Systems for the Tropics: The Example of Laser Cut Panels (Australia) and Plexiglas Daylight (Germany)." Seventh International IBPSA Conference, Anais, Rio de Janeiro, Brazil, August.

Lam R. W., E. M. Tan, L. N. Yatham, et al. 2001. "Seasonal Depression: The Dual Vulnerability Hypothesis Revisited." *Journal of Affective Disorders* 63: 123-132.

Landin-Wilhelmsen, K., L. Wilhelmsen, J. Wilske, et al. 1995. "Sunlight Increases Serum 25(OH) Vitamin D Concentration Whereas 1,25(OH) 2D3 Is Unaffected. Results from a General Population Study in Goteborg, Sweden (The WHO MONICA Project)." *European Journal of Clinical Nutrition* 49(6): 400-407.

Larkin, M., and M. D. Wilson. 1972. "Intensive Care Delirium: The Effect of Outside Deprivation in a Windowless Unit." *Archives of Internal Medicine* 130(2): 225-226.

Latour, A. 1991. *Louis I. Kahn, Writings, Lectures, Interviews*. New York: Rizzoli, 234, 252.

Lawrence Berkeley National Labs. 2013. Berkeley Lab Study Finds Big Energy Savings in the New York Times Building, http://newscenter.lbl.gov/news-releases/2013/02/05/new-york-times-building/ Feb 05, 2013.

Leahy, R. 2010. "The Cost of Depression." Huffington Post Blog.

Leblebici, D. 2012. "Impact of Workplace Quality on Employee's Productivity: A Case Study of a Bank in Turkey," *Journal of Business, Economics & Finance* 1(1): 38-49.

Le Corbusier. *Towards a New Architecture*, translated by J. Goodman (2007) from the 1928 printing of Le Corbusier, *Vers Une Architecture*, 2nd ed. (Paris: G. Cres, 1924), 102.

Le Corbusier. *Towards a New Architecture*, translated by F. Etchells from the 13th French edition. New York: Payson & Clarke, 29.

Lee, J. H., J. H. O'Keefe, D. D. Hensrud, and M. F. Holick. 2008. "Vitamin D Deficiency: An Important, Common, and Easily Treatable Cardiovascular Risk Factor?" *Journal of the American College of Cardiology* 52: 1949–1956.

Leger, D. 1994. "The Cost of Sleep-Related Accidents: A Report for the National Commission on Sleep Disorders Research." *Sleep* 17(1): 84–93.

Leppämäki, S., T. Partonen, O. Vakkuri, et al. 2003. "Effect of Controlled-Release Melatonin on Sleep Quality, Mood, and Quality of Life in Subjects with Seasonal or Weather-Associated Changes in Mood and Behaviour." *European Neuropsychopharmacology* 13(3): 137–145.

Leproult, R., G. Copinschi, O. Buxton, et al. 1997. "Sleep Loss Results in an Elevation of Cortisol Levels the Next Evening." *Sleep* 20: 865–870.

Lewy, A. J., T. A. Wehr, F. K. Goodwin, et al. 1980. "Light Suppresses Melatonin Secretion in Humans." *Science* 210: 1267–1269.

Lewy, A., H. Kern, N. Rosenthal, and T. Wehr. 1982. "Bright Artificial Light Treatment of a Manic-Depressive Patient with a Seasonal Mood Cycle." *Journal of Affective Disorders* 14: 13–19.

Li, D. H. W., J. C. Lam, and S. L. Wong. 2005. "Daylighting and Its Effects on Peak Load Determination." *Energy and Buildings* 30(10): 1817–1831.

Lighting Research Center (LRC). 2004. Daylighting Dividends.com.

Loftness, V., V. Hartkopf, B. Gurtekin, et al. 2003. "Linking Energy to Health and Productivity in the Built Environment." Center for Building Performance and Diagnostics, Carnegie Mellon, Greenbuild Conference, Pittsburgh, Pennsylvania, November 12-14.

Louis Harris & Associates. 1978. *The Steelcase National Study of Office Environments: Do They Work?* Grand Rapids, MI: Steelecase, Inc.

Luckiesh, M., and L. L. Holladay. 1925. "Glare and Visibility." *Transactions of the Illuminating Engneering Society, New York* 20(3): 221–252.

Luckiesh, M., and S. K. Guth. 1949. "Brightnesses in Visual Field at Borderline Between Comfort and Discomfort (BCD)." *Illuminating Engineering* 44: 650–670.

Ma, Y., P. Zhang, F. Wang, et al. 2011. "Association Between Vitamin D and Risk of Colorectal Cancer: A Systematic Review of Prospective Studies." *Journal of Clinical Oncology* 29(28): 3775–3782.

Magnusson, A., and T. Partonen. 2005 (August). "The Diagnosis, Symptomatology, and Epidemiology of Seasonal Affective Disorder." *CNS Spectrums* 10(8): 625–634.

Manning, P., ed. 1965. *Office Design: A Study of Environment*. Liverpool: University of Liverpool Press.

Marans, R. W., and K. F. Speckelmeyer. 1982. "Evaluating Open and Conventional Office Design." *Environment & Behavior* 14: 333–351.

Marcus, S. C., and M. Olfson. 2010 (December). "National Trends in the Treatment for Depression from 1998 to 2007." *Archives of General Psychiatry* 67(12): 1265–1273.

Melton, P. 2013. (March). "Healing Gardens Make Hospital Stays a Walk in the Park." BuildingGreen.com.

Ministère de l'Education. 1977. *Cahier des recommandations techniques de construction*. Editions du Service de l'Education Nationale, France.

Mistrick, R. G. 2006. "An Improved Procedure for Determining Skylight Well Efficiency Under Diffuse Glazing." *Journal of the Illuminating Engineering Society of North America* 2(4): 295–306.

Mitler, M.M., M. A. Carskadon, C. A. Czeisler, W. C. Dement, D. F. Dinges, and R. C. Graeber. 1988. "Catastrophes, Sleep, and Public Policy: Consensus Report." *Sleep* 11(1): 100–109.

Moon, P., and D. E. Spencer. 1942. "Illumination from a Non-Uniform Sky." *Illuminating Engineering* 37: 707–726.

Moss, T. H., and D. L. Sills. 1981. *The Three Mile Island Nuclear Accident: Lessons and Implications*. New York: New York Academy of Sciences.

Nabil, A., and J. Mardaljevic. 2005. "Useful Daylight Illuminance: A New Paradigm for Assessing Daylight in Buildings." *Lighting Research & Technology* 37: 41–57.

Nabil, A., and J. Mardaljevic. 2006. "Useful Daylight Illuminances: A Replacement for Daylight Factors." *Energy and Buildings* 38(7): 905–913.

Nayyar, K., and R. Cochrane. 1996 (May). "Seasonal Changes in Affective State Measured Prospectively and Retrospectively." *British Journal of Psychiatry* 168(5): 627–632.

Nazzal, A. A. 2001. "A New Daylight Glare Evaluation Method: Introduction of the Monitoring Protocol and Calculation Method." *Energy and Buildings* 3: 257–265.

NCSDS (National Commission on Sleep Disorders Research). 1994. *Wake Up America: A National Sleep Alert*. Volume 2 of Working Group Reports. Washington, DC: Government Printing Office. 331-355/30683.

Nebes, R. D., D. J. Buysse, E. M. Halligan, et al. 2008. "Self-Reported Sleep Quality Predicts Poor Cognitive Performance in Healthy Older Adults." *Journals of Gerontology* 64B(2): 180–187.

Ne'eman, E. 1977. "Sunlight Requirements in Buildings – Part 2." *Building and Environment* 11: 147–157.

Ne'eman, E., J. Cradock, and R. G. Hopkinson (1976). "Sunlight Requirements in Buildings – Part 1." *Building and Environment* 11: 217–238.

Ne'eman, E., W. Light, and R. G. Hopkinson. 1976. "Recommendations for the Admission of Sunlight in Buildings." *Building and Environment* 11(2): 91–101.

NTSB. "Grounding of the Liberian Passenger Ship Star Princess on Poundstone Rock, Lynn Canal, Alaska June 23, 1995: Marine Accident Report." 1997. Washington, DC: National Transportation Safety Board (accessed March 6, 2006). http://www.ntsb.gov/publictn/1997/MAR9702.pdf.

Oakley, G., S. B. Riffat, and L. Shao. 2000. "Daylighting Performance of Lightpipes." *Solar Energy* 69(2): 89–98.

Osler, M. 1993. *In the Eye of the Garden*. London: Weidenfeld & Nicolson.

Osterhaus, W. K. E. 1998. "Brightness as a Reliable and Simple Indicator for Discomfort Glare from Large Area Glare Sources." International Commission on Illumination (CIE), The First CIE Symposium on Lighting Quality, Vienna, Austria.

Osterhaus, W. K. E., and I. L. Bailey. 1992. "Large Area Glare Sources and Their Effect on Visual Discomfort and Visual Performance at Computer Stations." *Proceedings of the 1992 IEEE Applications Society Annual Meeting*, vol. 2, 1825–1829. Houston, TX.

Ottosson, J. 2001. "The Importance of Nature in Coping with a Crisis: A Photographic Essay." *Landscape Research* 26 (2) 165–172.

Pail, G., W. Huf, E. Pjrek, et al. 2011. "Bright-Light Therapy in the Treatment of Mood Disorders." *Neuropsychobiology* 64(3):152–162.

Paroncini, M., B. Calcagni, and F. Corvaro. 2007. "Monitoring of a Light-Pipe System." *Solar Energy* 81:1180–1186.

Petherbridge, P., and R. G. Hopkinson. 1950 Trans. *Illuminating Engineering Society*: 15, 39.

Pierson, J. 1995. "Letting the Sun Shine is Good for Business." *Wall Street Journal*, November 20, B1.

Prange, A. J., I. C. Wilson, C. W. Lynn, et al. 1974. "L-tryptophan in Mania: Contribution to a Permissive Hypothesis of Affective Disorders." *Archives of General Psychiatry* 30: 56–62.

Prasad G. V., M. M. Nash, and J. S. Zaltman. 2001. "Seasonal Variation in Outpatient Blood Pressure in Stable Renal Transplant Recipients." *Transplantation* 72(11): 1792–1794.

Pratt, L. A., and D. J. Brody. 2008. "Depression in the United States Household Population, 2005–2006." NCHS Data Brief Number 7.

Putrevu, S. 2001. "Exploring the Origin and Information Processing Differences Between Men and Women: Implications for Advertisers." *Journal of the Academy of Marketing Science* 10:124–136.

Qahtan, A., N. Keumala, S. P. Rao, and A. M. Alashwal. 2012. "A Case Study to Assess the Near-Glazed Workplace Thermal Performance." *Advanced Materials Research* 374-377:1724–1732.

Quartier, K., V. Jan, and K. Van Cleempoel. "The Interaction Between Interpreted Space, Mood and Behavior in Retail Environments: A Conceptual Research Model."

Raghuwanshi, A., et al. 2008. "Vitamin D and Multiple Sclerosis." *Journal of Cell Biochemistry* 105: 338.

Ramagopalan, S. V., et al. 2009. "Expression of the Multiple Sclerosis-Associated MHC Class II Allele HLA-DRB1*1501 Is Regulated by Vitamin D." *PLoS Genetics* 5:e1000369. http://www.plosgenetics.org/article/info:doi/10.1371/journal.pgen.1000369 (accessed July 26, 2010).

Reichel, H., H. P. Koeffler, and A. W. Norman. 1989. "The Role of Vitamin D Endocrine System in Health and Disease." *New England Journal of Medicine* 320: 980–991.

Reimann, G. 2010. "Managing Light and Daylight Efficiently for Tropical Office Buildings." Presentation at SB10SEA, KLCC Convention Centre, Malaysia, May 4, 2010.

Reinhart, C. F., and O. Walkenhorst. 2001. "Validation of Dynamic RADIANCE-Based Daylight Simulations for a Test Office with External Blinds." *Energy and Buildings* 33(7): 683–697.

Reinhart, C. F. 2005. "A Simulation-Based Review of the Ubiquitous Window-Head-Height to Daylight Zone Depth Rule-of-Thumb." Ninth International Building Performance Simulation Association (IBPSA) Conference, Montreal, August 15-18.

Reinhart, C. F., J. Mardaljevic, and Z. Rogers. 2006. "Dynamic Daylight Performance Metrics for Sustainable Building Design." *Leukos* 3(1): 7–31.

Romm, J. J. 1994. *Sustainable Building Technical Manual / Lean and Clean Management*. Kodansha America.

Romm, J. J., and W. D. Browning. 1994. *Greening the Building and the Bottom Line: Increasing Productivity Through Energy-Efficient Design*. Rocky Mountain Institute.

Rosenthal, N. E., D. A. Sack, J. C. Gillin, et al. 1984. "Seasonal Affective Disorder: A Description of the Syndrome and Preliminary Findings with Light Therapy." *Archives of General Psychiatry* 41(1): 72–80.

Rosenthal, N. E., C. J. Carpenter, S. P. James, B. et al. 1986. "Seasonal Affective Disorder in Children and Adolescents." *American Journal of Psychiatry* 143: 356–358.

Rudofsky, B. 1964. *Street for People: A Primer for Americans*. Garden City, NY: Doubleday.

Russel, J. A. 1980. "Circumplex Model of Affect." *Journal of Personality & Social Psychology* 39(6): 1161–1178.

Saadi, H. F., A. Adekunle Dawodu, B. O. Afandi, et al. 2007 (June). "Efficacy of Daily and Monthly High-Dose Calciferol in Vitamin D–Deficient Nulliparous and Lactating Women." *American Journal of Clinical Nutrition* 85(6): 1565–1571.

Salterpilon.com. http://www.salterpilon.com/projects/healthcare/thunder-bay-regional-health-sciences-centre (accessed December 2013).

Saxon, R. 1983. *Atrium Buildings: Development and Design*. New York: Van Nostrand Reinhold, 55–64, 73-76.

Scartezzini, J. L., and G. Courret. 2002. "Anidolic Daylighting Systems." *Solar Energy* 73(2): 123–135.

Schleithoff, S. S., A. Zittermann, B. Stuttgen, et al. 2003. "Low Levels of Intact Osteocalcin in Patients with Congestive Heart Failure." *Journal of Bone and Mineral Metabolism* 21: 247–252.

Schweitzer, M., L. Gilpin, and S. Frampt. 2004. "Healing Spaces: Elements of Environmental Design That Make an Impact on Health." *Journal of Alternative and Complementary Medicine* 10(supplement 1): 71–83.

Searles, H. F. 1960. *The Nonhuman Environment in Normal Development in Schizophrenia.* New York: International University Press.

Shane, E., D. Mancini, K. Aaronson, et al. 1997. "Bone Mass, Vitamin D Deficiency, and Hyperparathyroidism in Congestive Heart Failure." *American Journal of Medicine* 103: 197–207.

Sigurdson, K., and N. Ayas. 2007. "The Public Health and Safety Consequences of Sleep Disorders." *Canadian Journal of Physioogy andl Pharmacology* 85: 179–183.

Skouteris, H., C. Germano, E. H. Wertheim, et al. 2008. "Sleep Quality and Depression During Pregnancy: A Prospective Study." *Journal of Sleep Research* 17(2): 217–220.

Smith, G. B. 2004 (October). "Materials and Systems for Efficient Lighting and Delivery of Daylight." *Solar Energy Materials and Solar Cells* 84(1–4): 395–409.

Smolders, J., et al. 2009. "Vitamin D Status Is Positively Correlated with Regulatory T Cell Function in Patients with Multiple Sclerosis." *PLoS One* 4:e6635. http://www.plosone.org/article/info:-doi/10.1371/journal.pone.0006635 (accessed March 1, 2013).

Song, K. D. 2007. "Influence of Canopy Systems on Daylight Performance of Four-Sided Atria Under an Overcast Sky." *Indoor and Built Environment* 16(2): 110–120.

Southern California Edison. 2008. "Office of the Future Phase II Report: The 25% Solution." Office of the Future Consortium. ET 08.01.

Spiegel, K., R. Leproult, and E. Van Cauter. 1999. "Impact of Sleep Debt on Metabolic and Endocrine Function." *Lancet* 354: 1435–1439.

Spiegel, K., E. Tasali, P. Penev, et al. 2004. "Sleep Curtailment in Healthy Young Men Is Associated with Decreased Leptin Levels, Elevated Ghrelin Levels and Increased Hunger and Appetite." *Annals of Internal Medicine* 141: 846–850.

Stenzel, A. G. 1962. "Erfahrungen mit 1000 lx in einer Lederwarenfabrik" (Experiences with 1000 lx in a leather factory)." *Lichttechnick* 14: 16–18.16.

Stewart, W. F., J. A. Ricci, E. Chee, et al. 2003. "Cost of Lost Productive Work Time Among US Workers with Depression." *Journal of the American Medical Association* 289: 3135–3144.

Stigsdotter, U., and P. Grahn. 2002. "What Makes a Garden a Healing Garden?" *Journal of Therapeutic Horticulture* 13: 60–69.

Sullivan, B., and W. T. Payne. 2007. "Affective Disorders and Cognitive Failures: A Comparison of Seasonal and Nonseasonal Depression." *American Journal of Psychiatry* 164: 1663–1667.

Sun Han, K., L. Kim, and I. Shim. 2012 (December). "Stress and Sleep Disorder." *Experimental Neurobiology* 21(4): 141–150.

Sundstrom, E. D. 1986. *Work Places: The Psychology of the Physical Environment in Offices and Factories.* Cambridge and New York: Cambridge University Press.

Sundstrom, E. D., R. E. Burt, and D. Kamp. 1980. "Privacy at Work: Architectural Correlates of Job Satisfaction and Job Performance." *Academy of Management Journal* 23: 101–117.

Taheri, S., L. Lin, D. Austin, et al. 2004. "Short Sleep Duration Is Associated with Reduced Leptin, Elevated Ghrelin, and Increased Body Mass Index (BMI)." *PLOS Medicine* 27: A146–A147.

Tennessen, C. M., and B. Cimprich. 1995. "Views to Nature: Effects on Attention." *Journal of Environmental Psychology* 15: 77–85.

Terman, M., J. S. Terman, F. M. Quitkin, et al. 1989. "Light Therapy for Seasonal Affective Disorder. A Review of Efficacy." *Neuropsychopharmacology* 2: 1–22.

Thayer, B. M. 1995. "Daylighting and Productivity at Lockeed." *Solar Today.* May/June.

Thompson, C., and G. Isaacs. 1988. "Seasonal Affective Disorder – A British Sample Symptomatology in Relation to Mode of Referral and Diagnostic Subtype." *Journal of Affective Disorders* 14(1): 1–12.

Tsangrassoulis, A., and M. Santamouris. 2000. "A Method to Estimate the Daylight Efficiency of Round Skylights." *Energy and Buildings* 32: 41–45.

Tuaycharoen, N., and P. R. Tregenza. 2005. "Discomfort Glare from Interesting Images." *Lighting Research and Technology* 37(4): 329–341.

Ulrich, R. S. 1984. "View Through a Window May Influence Recovery from Surgery." *Science* 224: 420–421.

Ulrich, R. S., R. F. Simons, B. D. Losito, et al. 1991. "Stress Recovery During Exposure to Natural and Urban Environments." *Journal of Environmental Psychology* 11: 201–230.

"United States Department of Energy. 2008 (October). "Energy Efficiency Trends in Residential and Commercial Buildings," Report. http://apps1.eere.energy.gov/buildings/publications/pdfs/corporate/bt_stateindustry.pdf (accessed March 2013).

United States Nuclear Regulatory Commission (USNRC). 1987. *Report on the Accident at the Chernobyl Nuclear Power Station.* Washington, DC: Government Printing Office. NU-REG 1250.

United States Senate Committee on Energy and National Resources. 1986. *The Chernobyl Accident.* Washington, DC: Government Printing Office.

Veitch, J. A., and G. R. Newsham. 1998 (winter). "Determinants of Lighting Quality I: State of the Science." *Journal of the Illuminating Engineering Society* 27: 92–106.

Vitruvius, *Ten Books on Architecture,* translated by M. H. Morgan. 2002. New York: Dover Publications, Book 1, Chapter 2, 13–16.

Vittori, G., and A. Fitch. 2008. "The AMD Lone Star Campus: Assessing Green Strategies, Report for the Center for Maximum Potential Building Systems."

Walch, J. M., B. S. Rabin, R. Day, et al. 2005. "The Effect of Sunlight on Postoperative Analgesic Medication Use: A Prospective Study of Patients Undergoing Spinal Surgery." *Psychosomatic Medicine* 67(1): 156–163.

Waldram, P. J. 1950. *A Measuring Diagram for Daylight Illumination.* London: B.T. Batsford.

Wang, N., and M. Boubekri. 2010. "Investigation of Declared Sitting Preference and Measured Cognitive Performance in a Sunlit Room." *Journal of Environmental Psychology* 30(2): 226–238.

Wang, N., and M. Boubekri. 2012. "Daylight's Influence Beyond Our Eyes: Investigating the Mediating role of Mood in Cognitive Performance in a Sunlit Workplace." *Light & Engineering* 3.

Watson, D., L. A. Clark, and A. Tellegen. 1988. "Development and Validation of Brief Measures of Positive and Negative Affect: The PANAS Scales." *Journal of Personality and Social Psychology* 54(6): 1063–1070.

Wayne, B. J., and A. C. Ronald. 2004. "Toward Optimal Healing Environments in Health Care." *Journal of Alternative and Complementary Medicine:* 1–6.

Webb A. R., C. Pillbeam, N. Hanafin, and M. F. Holick. 1990 (June). "An Evaluation of the Relative Contribution of Exposure to Sunlight and of Diet to the Circulating Concentration of 25-Hydroxyvitamin D in an Elderly Nursing Home Population in Boston." *American Journal of Clinical Nutrition* 51(6): 1075–1081.

Welford, W. T., and R. Winston. 1989. *Non-Imaging Optics.* New York: Academic Press.

Weston, H. C. 1922. *A Study of the Efficiency in Fine Linen-Weaving.* London: His Majesty's Stationery Office.

Williams, A., B. Atkinson, K. Garbesi, and F. Rubinstein. 2011 (September). "A Meta-Analysis of Energy Savings from Lighting Controls in Commercial Buildings," Report, Energy Analysis Department, Lawrence Berkeley National Laboratory, Berkeley, CA.

Wineman, J. D. 1982. "Office Design and Evaluation: An Overview." *Environment and Behavior* 14(3): 271–298.

Wirz-Justice, A., P. Graw, K. Krauchi, and H. R. Wacker. 2003. "Seasonality in Affective Disorders in Switzerland." *Acta Psychiatrica Scandanavica* 108 (Supplement 418): 92–95.

Wood, B., Rea, M. S., B. Plitnick, and M. G. Figueiro. 2013 (March). "Light Level and Duration of Exposure Determine the Impact of Self-Luminous Tablets on Melatonin Suppression." *Applied Ergonomics* 44(2): 237–40.

Wurtman, R. J. 1975. "The Effects of Light on the Human Body." *Scientific American* 233(1): 68–77.

Yildirim, K., A. Akalin-Baskayab, and M. Celebia. 2007. "The Effects of Window Proximity, Partition Height, and Gender on Perceptions of Open-Plan Offices." *Journal of Environmental Psychology* 27: 154–165.

Yildirim K., A. Akalin-Baskaya, and M. L. Hidayetoglu. 2007. "Effects of Indoor Color on Mood and Cognitive Performance." *Building and Environment* 42(9): 3233–3240.

Yun, G. Y., J. Y. Shin, and J. T. Kim. 2010. "Influence of Window Views on the Subjective Evaluation of Discomfort Glare." Third International Symposium on Sustainable Healthy Buildings, Seoul, Korea, May 27.

Zeller, W. 2011 (May). "UKP NESK: TNT Green Office in Hoofddorp, Holland." *REHVA Journal,* 66–72.

Zhang, X., and T. Muneer. 2005. "A Design Guide for Performance Assessment of Solar Light-Pipes." *Lighting Research and Technology* 34(2): 149–169.

Index

ALANOD GmbH & Co. KG

Daylight creates wellbeing, daylight synchronizes our body clock.
Systems designed with highly reflective MIRO-SILVER® surfaces from ALANOD are more efficient and allow smaller components.
Thus, the daylight-based heat input is reduced by one third, which has a positive effect on both; the building air conditioning requirements and the end-users.
www.alanod.com

Bartenbach®

Bartenbach GmbH

Bartenbach is a global market leader for day- and artificial lighting design. Bartenbach strives to develop and design high-quality lighting solutions based on the visual and biological light requirements of building users.
„Not from the luminaire to the overall appearance, but rather from the desired ambience to a lighting concept based on the principles of visual perception. Only then will we arrive at a suitable luminaire or lighting system, applying our knowledge of physics and lighting technology."
Christian Bartenbach
www.bartenbach.com

durlum GmbH

durlum develops and manufactures innovative metal ceilings, lighting and daylight systems for architectural applications worldwide. We work with our project partners on solutions that create a perfect combination between function and design.
Solutions to make you feel at home.
www.durlum.com